The Pocket Essential

TERRY PRATCHETT

First published in Great Britain 2001 by Pocket Essentials, 18 Coleswood Road,
Harpenden, Herts, AL5 1EQ

Distributed in the USA by Trafalgar Square Publishing, PO Box 257, Howe Hill
Road, North Pomfret, Vermont 05053

A CIP catalogue record for this book is available from the British Library.

ISBN 1-903047-39-0

9 8 7 6 5 4 3

Book typeset by Pdunk
Printed and bound by Cox & Wyman

To Edward and Farah

Acknowledgements

Many thanks as always to the Prefab Four (and the fifth Prefab, Tanya Brown) for their oval influences and their temptations (alcoholic, epicural, cultural, anything that involves spending money really) to take the weekend off when I should have been buried in writing this. Thanks guys. Paul Duncan was generous with deadlines, and I'd like to thank him for his work on the three Pocket Essentials I've done. Apologies must go to Xavier Mendik, whom I entirely failed to meet up with during the writing of this book, though not for want of trying. I think I've a window in August – how about you? I'd like to thank various colleagues at BCUC, especially Caroline Bainbridge and John Mercer who have to endure sharing an office with me. Mark Bould was very clear that he didn't have anything to do with this book. Hopefully he'll think this one adequate too. Thanks, again, to Robert Edgar who accompanied me to the conference in Sheffield on Bakhtin which finally convinced me that there were things to be said about Terry Pratchett beyond stating the obvious. Edward James and Farah Mendlesohn published the resulting article in *Foundation*, and then invited me to co-edit *Guilty Of Literature*; obviously all the contributors to that volume should check that I haven't ripped off too many of their ideas. Thanks to Brian Ameringen for adding more caveats to my emptor. Terry Pratchett's agent Colin Smythe generously read through the manuscript and clarified a number of points and corrected others. Any errors which remain are naturally my own.

Anyone who writes on Terry Pratchett clearly owes a huge debt to his creations, and risks accusations of jumping on a bandwagon of a publishing phenomenon. Mr Pratchett allows groups to perform plays based on his works in return for making a donation to the Orangutan Foundation. In keeping with the spirit of this practice, I am donating half of any money I make from this project to the same charity.

CONTENTS

Introduction

In Britain it has been estimated that 10% of all books sold are fantasy. And of that fantasy, 10% is written by Terry Pratchett. So, do the sums: 1% of all books sold in Britain are written by Terry Pratchett. Coo. He's achieved such figures with the aid of very enthusiastic booksellers, excited readers, and librarians who knew a good thing when they saw one. The serious press kept away, except to sneer, although most reviewers enjoyed whatever book it was they eventually read (although they are contractually obligated to mention anoraks in their review). But whether the books were being reviewed or not, from the late 1980s onwards each hardback hit the top ten chart as it was released, and repeated the feat with the paperback edition. When the maps were finally drawn and published, these even entered the non-fiction charts. There have been radio serialisations, TV adaptations, numerous plays, dozens of audiobooks, pottery figures, calendars, diaries, an encyclopaedia, a couple of computer games, a quiz book, a CD of music inspired by the *Discworld*, several fanzines, newsgroups, fanclubs and a couple of *Discworld* conventions. There was even a whole volume of criticism discussing his work. And this one makes it two.

Not bad for a writer who only published four novels in the first two decades of his career. Still, he has made up for this with over thirty in the next two.

Before The Discworld

Terry Pratchett might be seen as a child prodigy who was a late developer. Born in Beaconsfield, England, in 1948, he had his first short story 'The Hades Business' published in a school magazine and then in *Science Fantasy* in 1963. His second story 'Night Dweller' was in *New Worlds* in 1965. 'The Hades Business' is a variation on the pact with the Devil, in which the Devil comes to make a deal with Crucible, an advertiser or what we now think of as a public relations consultant. Hell is in the doldrums, and the Devil wants to jazz up its reputation. After initial reluctance, Crucible agrees, and succeeds, but now the rebranded hell is too noisy and the Devil repents, ascending to heaven. Usually it's the mortal who should read the small print in the demonic contract and end up being damned, but here the positions are changed, with Crucible coming remarkably well out of the deal. The Devil ends his ways and returns to heaven, rather than the Faustian narrative of the mortal dragged off to Hell. Most of the story is dialogue and the Voice of God speaks in italicised capital letters – perhaps a distant precursor of one of Pratchett's most popular characters, Death.

Pratchett also wrote a lot of material for newspapers, much of it pseudonymous, and even he doesn't know how much short fiction has appeared by him alongside news reports. He is also a talented cartoonist, having produced sketches of the characters in *The Carpet People* as they developed and designing the covers for his first few novels. Some of his cartoons also appeared in periodicals, including the Warlock Hall cartoons in *The Psychic Researcher & Spiritualist Gazette*.

Pratchett had the decency to wait until his twenties before getting his first novel, *The Carpet People* (1971), published with Colin Smythe Ltd, a small publishing house based in Gerrards Cross. The novel had been written by the author when he was seventeen years old, and was published after a conversation with the publisher when Pratchett was working as a journalist. (When the novel was republished in 1992 it was in a revised form). Pratchett's duties on the *Bucks Free Press*, *Western Daily Herald* and the *Bath Chronicle* gave him little time to write his own fiction, so his second novel, *The Dark Side Of The Sun* didn't appear until 1976 and the third, *Strata*, was published in 1981. By then Pratchett had become a publicity officer for the Central Electricity Generating Board.

Terry Pratchett could have become just another SF writer who produced a handful of novels (or even just a couple of short stories) and then have been forgotten by all but the amateur bibliographers of SF fandom. In his three novels Pratchett had shown a talent for parody, particular of the kind of narrative which involved the discovery of a large mysterious artefact – which critic Roz Kaveney dubbed the Big Dumb Object. A number of authors wrote such novels in the early 1970s. Most famously, Larry Niven's *Ringworld* (1970) was set on a world a million miles wide curved into a loop millions of miles in circumference. Niven's brand of hard science fiction prides itself upon its scientific accuracy (in this case scuppered by the Earth rotating in the wrong direction in the first edition), and the Ringworld proved to be an unstable object; further novels allowed Niven to reveal various stabilising devices. More stable was the Dyson Sphere, in effect an artificial hollow earth: the scientist Freeman J Dyson postulated the manufacture of a thin planetary shell so large that a sun could be put inside it. The inhabitants would live on the interior surface. Bob Shaw's *Orbitsville* (1975) is the classic examination of this idea.

Both *The Dark Side Of The Sun* and *Strata* owe much to Niven's science fiction, but something was clearly special about the world Pratchett created in the latter novel: a flat planet in a Ptolemaic universe. Of course, Pratchett hadn't invented the idea: Hindu mythology offers the clearest version (of several) of a flat planet perched on the backs of elephants stood on the back of a tortoise. Here Pratchett was able to use a mythical idea – along with several other myths – to produce an SF novel, working out what mechanisms were necessary to support such a planet.

But there was more mileage in the idea. People had believed that the world was flat, despite all evidence to the contrary. (Well, actually a number of civilisations had established the spherical nature of the planet, but we're talking about Europe, which is clearly the only civilisation that matters). In *Strata* the idea was explored from the outside. How would the planet feel to someone who had grown up with a flat planet as reality? What about a world where belief became central to existence – to the extent that dragons existed because of people's beliefs?

To do this, the genre had to be fantasy rather than science fiction, and the parodic quotient was to be upped.

Fantasy

Fantasy has always been with us – it forms the bedrock of myths, creation legends and tall tales told around the fire. In fact tales in which deeds were exaggerated into heroism and enemies made into monsters were probably more often told than tales which attempted to depict the world as it really was. However, it's not until the middle of the eighteenth century, that it actually makes sense to speak of fantasy. During this period printing technology, increased leisure time for an emerging middle class, and the new phenomenon called capitalism combined to allow novels to be published in greater numbers than ever before, and at greater length. As the three-volume or triple-decker novel emerged as the preferred literary form, the trend was towards novels which depicted a cross-section of society, with consistent space and time, unique events, unique characters and plausible action. Yet at the same time as realism settled the novel down, there was a boom in the Gothic novel, which featured superstition, excitement, thrills, craggy landscapes, simpering heroines, evil villains, incest and dark deeds. It was the realist novel that won critical respectability through the nineteenth century – Austen over the Brontës – but otherwise realist novelists like Charles Dickens and Wilkie Collins were happy to play with Gothic elements in their stories. At the end of the nineteenth century the pendulum swung back to shorter fictions with elements of the uncanny – Robert Louis Stevenson's *Strange Case Of Dr Jekyll And Mr Hyde* (1886), Oscar Wilde's *The Picture Of Dorian Gray* (1891) and Bram Stoker's *Dracula* (1897) among others. But Stevenson and Stoker were both too popular to be taken seriously by critics for the best part of a century, and everyone knew that *Dorian Gray* was pure filth.

Sometime around the First World War, a South African-born philologist was playing with invented languages and started developing narratives that could contain them. After numerous false starts, he realised that his mythic material was best deployed as a background of which his characters were aware, whilst the reader's interest was held by a quest narrative. The first volume to be published was *The Hobbit* (1937) and the author was JRR Tolkien. The book was a success, and a sequel followed: *The Lord Of The Rings* (1954-1955), a triple-decker fantasy novel. There had been other fantasies, of course, but none quite as successful in terms of the richness of their imagined worlds or the number of copies sold. The success became a phenomenon when a pirated edition appeared in America in the 1960s, and the ecological subtext became part of the credo of American students and hippies, much to the horror of the rather conservative Tolkien.

Imitators followed, but none with quite the same success. By the late 1970s, the genre was dominated by mix-and-match fantasy trilogies full of heroes, magic swords, impossible quests, jaw-splitting place names, and bad poetry. *The Lord Of The Rings* had been parodied, of course (e.g. National Lampoon's *Bored Of The Rings*), but fantasy in general was open to a kind of light-hearted critique, one which would skewer some of the idiocies of fantasy – what Conan the Barbarian (created by Robert E Howard by in stories written between 1932 and 1936) might get up to in later life if his career was as long as his creator's successors made it, how dragons might survive, and how magic might work in context. At the same time, it would play fair, it would work as a fantasy novel.

The Discworld And Its Sequences

Pratchett did this in *The Colour Of Magic* (1983) and again in *The Light Fantastic* (1986), putting an outsider figure (Twoflower, a tourist with a distinct Japanese edge to his character) into an unfamiliar city with an inept wizard (Rincewind, a name borrowed from the humorist Beachcomber) as his unwilling guide. In *Lord Of The Rings* Gandalf was such an authority figure and so powerful that he had to be killed off by a Balrog to allow some sense of tension to the narrative. However, Rincewind is so helplessly powerless that any spell he might possibly cast is more likely to kill than to save them. In the early novels featuring Rincewind it was explained that he had inadvertently learned one of the eight major spells, which had prevented him from learning any more.

In 1987, Pratchett was finally able to become a full-time freelance writer, and he shifted from having Colin Smythe as a publisher to Colin Smythe as an agent. He began to produce at least one a year, with Gollancz publishing the novels in hardback, in association with Colin Smythe Ltd until *Sourcery* (1988), and Corgi publishing them in paperback. Sales slowly climbed, helped in part by readings of *The Colour Of Magic* and *Equal Rites* (1987) on *Woman's Hour*, Terry's unisex name allegedly gaining him a female as well as a male following. The readings won both praise and hostility.

Obviously Pratchett could not write half a dozen parodies of *The Lord Of The Rings* or even fantasy in general; he certainly could not do it twenty-five times or more. To continue, further topics would have to become grist to his mill; the all-male world of wizardry could be critiqued by offering a female wizard's experiences, the character of Death could be expanded and examined, and so on. The two novels *Wyrd Sisters* (1988) and *Pyramids* (1989) signpost the way forward. The witch from *Equal Rites* was joined with two others to form a coven, in a parody of *Macbeth*, whilst the action moved from Ankh-Morpork to the kingdom of Lancre to offer a retelling of a regicide, this time as comedy. As a narrative it could work – ambitious husband and scheming wife murder a king with hilarious consequences – but the audience is too likely to know the ending. OK, so splice in Shakespeare's other homicidal classic, *Hamlet*, and you also shift the moral centre, away from the murderer – which would be awkward for all but the darkest comedies – to the exposure of the murder plot. The play within the play of *Hamlet*, which offers a commentary on theatre, can also be played for laughs (see *A Midsummer Night's Dream*, used in *Lords And Ladies*), but why not have the playwright not devising alternates to Shakespeare's canon, but rather classic Hollywood comedies?

Pyramids pushed the action even further away from the known Discworld, to a fantasy-land equivalent of Egypt. Of course, most of us only know Egypt through versions of *The Mummy* and holiday programmes, so there's no need for any in-depth research. The writer can play on the reader's knowledge of Egypt as much as parodying fantasy. Perhaps a useful comparison can be made with the *Carry On* series of films, such as *Carry On Cleo* (1964), *Carry On Doctor* (1968) and *Carry On Up The Khyber* (1968). None of these films are dependent on a detailed knowledge of Cleopatra, the workings of the NHS or the British Empire to work as comedies, rather they require a specialised setting to act as a backdrop to a rather limited repertoire of routines – ineffectual authority figures, heroic underdogs, frigid matriarchs, dirty old men, nymphomaniacs and so forth – and endless puns and double entendres. In retrospect, they do offer a commentary of sorts (perhaps not intended) on Cleopatra, the NHS and so on, and on British attitudes towards class, sex, gender relations and so forth. But if Pratchett could rework Egypt, then he could rework China (*Interesting Times*, 1994) and Australia (*The Last Continent*, 1998). Hollywood comedy could be followed by references to Hollywood in general (*Moving Pictures*, 1990), rock music (*Soul Music*, 1994), opera (*Maskerade*, 1995) and so on.

Much of the humour depends on having two ideas in mind at once. At a trivial level this might be two words being confused for each other, as in the endless, cross-purposes discussions of the wizards or the double entendres of Nanny Ogg, or Mort's confusion between broth and brothel (and later on Carrot's naïve renting of a room with Mrs Palm, among a large number of young women and numerous gentleman callers). It might be a familiar concept, but viewed in the context of a fantasy world. Assassins have to be trained, and their final examination may indeed be like a driving test. We're aware of the real-world parallels, but crucially for the humour the characters are not. (I feel that some of the early novels have too many overt references to the real world, which risks destroying the illusion.)

Partly, perhaps, because of the necessity for the central characters not to know quite what is going on, Pratchett has often used a child, childlike or teenaged protagonist: Rincewind and Twoflower in different ways in the first two books, Esk in *Equal Rites*, Mort in *Mort* (1987), to some extent Coin in *Sourcery* (1988), Teppic in *Pyramids*, Carrot in *Guards! Guards!* (1989) and Brutha in *Small Gods* (1992). A lot of comedy can be derived from the mismatch between vaulting ambition, and falling over having mistimed the jump, from the difference between the desire for something or someone, and the failure to attain the heart's desire. Success is not particularly funny. Walking is not funny. Walking and slipping over on a banana skin is funny (well, maybe not *that* funny, but it's a start). The innocent abroad is able to fail in such a way that we feel sympathy for their plight whilst laughing at and with them. At the same time their innocence rather than ignorance seems to operate as some kind of talisman, and disarms any opponent. The powerful brought low by the powerless, the master beaten by the servant and the thief conned by his intended victim are all sources of comedy. And then, the hero or heroine comes to maturity or adulthood and finally wins the girl or the boy and the narrative ends, often with a marriage or the achievement of the heart's desire. So what happens next? Well, there's always another innocent to write about.

Perhaps. But then there is a certain amount of diminishing returns here, and a prolific author can't just go on creating characters who are used only once. In the early books which feature the Unseen University, there appears to be a different cast of wizards each time, certainly a different Archchancellor, with the Librarian who has been turned into an orangutan (or orangutan, depending on which book you are reading) as the only constant – indeed, the Librarian appears in most of the books even if the other wizards don't. By the time of *Moving Pictures*, the wizardly personnel settle down.

We don't get to see Mort again, but his daughter Susan appears twice, in *Soul Music* and *Hogfather* (1996). In the former Pratchett even takes the brave step of killing off Mort.

This recycling of characters means that sequences can be discerned within the series. These overlap but broadly speaking there are the wizards/ Rincewind, the witches/Granny Weatherwax, Death and the City Watch/ Vimes. This listing excludes *Pyramids, Moving Pictures* and *Small Gods*, the first and third of which together with *Hogfather* have been released as the Gods trilogy (2000); *The Truth* (2000) is only marginally a City Watch novel. It might be helpful to think of the sequences as explorations of individual themes.

The wizard sequence – *The Colour Of Magic*, *The Light Fantastic*, *Equal Rites* (partly), *Sourcery*, *Eric* (1990), *Reaper Man* (1991), *Soul Music*, *Interesting Times*, *The Last Continent* and *The Science Of Discworld* (1999) – all feature wizards or the Unseen University (an echo of the Invisible College of Elizabethan magician and mystic, John Dee?) as central characters or location. Aside from a female wizard in *The Colour Of Magic*, the housekeeper Mrs Whitlow and Esk, the world of the wizards is an entirely male one—they live a monastic existence largely built around eating and pointless arguments. In many ways they owe a debt to the schoolmasters of *Gormenghast* rather than to the campus novels of David Lodge or Malcolm Bradbury. Pratchett's use of the word 'faculty' to refer to the wizards, and the constant contact with the Archchancellor, rather than a focus on one faculty out of several, suggests an unfamiliarity with current tertiary education practice. Aside from occasionally summoning Death (who appears to wizards on their death anyway) and trying to track down Rincewind, it's rare that we see wizards using magic. When they do, it is invariably disastrous.

The witches are easily distinguished from the sex-starved patriarchs who are wizards; sexuality is closer to their magic or their actions. Wizardly magic comes from the skies, witch magic comes from the Earth. Again, though, it is rare that the witches resort to magic. Granny Weatherwax is a believer in headology, using people's prejudices, preconceptions and beliefs against them. We see three different types of women as witches: the maiden with the power of possibility, the mother with the power of the matriarch, and the crone with the power of knowledge. In the Witches sequence we see these powers in flux and flow – *Equal Rites*, *Wyrd Sisters*, *Witches Abroad* (1991), *Lords And Ladies* (1992), *Maskerade* and *Carpe Jugulum* (1998). Granny Weatherwax is the crone, although few call her such to her face, Nanny Ogg the mother, with a vast extended family and a line in innuendo, and Magrat Garlick the naïve maiden, with book learning rather than experience. Over the course of the books Magrat Garlick becomes romantically attached to King Verence, and this means she has to be swept away as a character, having achieved the desire. A new maiden is quickly forthcoming in *Maskerade*. But Pratchett wisely can't throw a character away after ten years; Magrat has metamorphosed off-stage into a mother, and Nanny can be promoted to crone, with the inevitable sidelining of Granny Weatherwax. Having created a character as an old woman, Pratchett will have to deal with old age and death. The point of being a witch is knowing when to use power, and Weatherwax is often to be found at the heart of a debate about good and evil. Her grandmother and sister went to the dark side, Granny could follow suit. As she learns from Mightily Oats in *Carpe Jugulum* it's not necessarily action which counts, but the intention behind it.

The Death sequence – *Mort*, *Reaper Man*, *Soul Music*, *Hogfather* – focuses in some way on work practices. *Mort* begins with Death trying to find an apprentice, with Death presumably aware that he is not going to be in the job forever. Indeed, in *Reaper Man*, Death finds himself made redundant, and discovers that there aren't that many openings for a dab hand with the scythe. In *Soul Music* and *Hogfather*, his granddaughter Susan ends up taking over the family business for varying reasons, and a very reluctant Death she is too. Of course, Death is the only character to appear in all of the *Discworld* novels, and he's to be found in some of the non-*Discworld* works as well.

Perhaps the most unexpected and most satisfying sequence is the last to emerge, the City Watch (also referred to as the Guards books or the Night Watch books): *Guards! Guards!*, *Men At Arms* (1993), *Feet Of Clay* (1996), *Jingo* (1997), *The Fifth Elephant* (1999) and *The Truth*. These are the most political of the novels, and involve a debate around who should hold power. Captain Samuel Vimes, later Commander Vimes, later than that knighted and even later still ennobled, is an alcoholic chief of police, who owes more than a little to the American hard-boiled tradition of detecting. He hates all races and species equally, and is determined to do right despite the fact that this will bring him into direct conflict with the city he was employed to serve. The head of Ankh-Morpork, Patrician Vetinari, had reckoned that if there had to be crime, then it had better be organised, and made thievery and assassination the responsibility of the appropriate guilds. Vimes can only officially deal with crimes that fall outside guild jurisdiction – the guilds being much more intolerant of unlicensed thieving. Still, Vimes is kept busy with a series of homicides by conspirators who either want to re-establish the lost king of Ankh-Morpork (Vimes' ancestor having dispatched the last) or remove Vetinari. In later books like *Jingo* and *The Fifth Elephant* he is manipulated to do Vetinari's bidding by dealing with war or diplomacy, flip sides of the same coin. He is also the long-suffering victim of Vetinari's equal opportunity policies, having to deal with dwarfs, trolls, gargoyles and other species in the multi-ethnic Watch. One such minority is Corporal (later Captain) Carrot, a human raised by a dwarf, and possibly heir to the throne of Ankh-Morpork, and a policeman in the tradition of *Dixon Of Dock Green*.

Other Works

Pratchett has produced other books as well, *The Unadulterated Cat* (1989), illustrated by Gray Jolliffe, and *Good Omens* (1990), a novel co-written with Neil Gaiman, being notable. He has enjoyed a long collaboration with Stephen Briggs, who has adapted a number of Pratchett's novels into plays, some of which can be purchased in book form and then performed, on payment of a donation to the Orangutan Foundation. Briggs has collaborated more equally on three of the four maps (having convinced Pratchett that a map was possible) and on *The Discworld Companion* (1994). Briggs probably knows more about the Discworld than Pratchett does. Which is all rather worrying. Briggs was also involved in *Nanny Ogg's Cookbook* (1999).

Pratchett has also produced two trilogies for children, *The Bromeliad* (1989-90) and *The Johnny Maxwell Trilogy* (1992-96), both discussed at length in Chapter Three. *The Bromeliad* is science fiction masquerading as fantasy, and features heroes (both male and female) who didn't set out to be heroes or leaders, but nevertheless lead others to safety. Johnny Maxwell is another hero despite himself, saving a race of aliens, helping the local dead and confronting Second World War history. The trilogy also makes points about racism and sexism, without glibly suggesting that any person who commits such acts is wrong.

Power

In Pratchett's universe power corrupts and absolute power corrupts absolutely. The potentially most powerful characters on Discworld are the wizards of the Unseen University, but fortunately they are either too busy fighting their way up the greasy poles of the university power structure (initially at least for each wizard there is another eight below him, but since that makes well over two million wizards that has to be wrong) or too busy being lazy to do any real damage. The exception to this rule is in *Sourcery*, when they decide they want to have their due respect from their host city—never have town and gown been so dangerously poised at each others' throats.

Equally the witches have power, mostly psychological – headology – which could be disastrous in the wrong hands. I've already noted that Granny Weatherwax could easily go over to the dark side; when the teenage girls in *Lords And Ladies* grapple with forces beyond their understanding, evil is let into the Discworld. Nanny has powers relating to birth, is very much part of her community (if only because she is related to so much of it) and rules her sons and daughters-in-law with a rod of iron, metaphorically speaking. Granny has powers relating to death (although she is also skilled in midwifery), and is on the edge of the community.

Death, too, has power and responsibility, a responsibility to do his job. Whilst the death of kittens is clearly an emotional wrench, he has learnt that death is a natural process and not necessarily a bad thing; the impact of somebody's death may in fact change things for the better. Most deaths occur naturally (or rather without his intervention) but he does attend wizards, kings, witches, and anyone else he has taken an interest in. And after death, it's up to the individual whether heaven or hell awaits, or just nothingness. In recent books there has been a sense of death being more to do with probability, with a couple of characters poised on the edge of dying – and since these have involved major characters it seems likely that Pratchett may kill off one of his heroes. Indeed the logic of the witches sequence all but demands that he kills off Granny Weatherwax, which he comes close to in *Carpe Jugulum*.

Captain Carrot is just one of what seems like several dozen long-lost heirs to power, and shows no sign of wishing to take the throne of Ankh-Morpork. He does have considerable power to command the denizens of that great city. Across in Lancre, a long-lost heir to the throne refuses to take on the rôle, instead a fool becomes king, and Verence II is by all accounts a successful monarch, having not really sought power for himself.

Patrician Havelock Vetinari – a bit like the Abbot in *The Bromeliad* – is someone who has sought power, and he'd probably have Machiavelli's *The Prince* at his bedside for a little light reading. He has a background in juggling and training from the Assassin's Guild, but little is known about his past. It has to be admitted that he has brought a kind of status quo to the city, maintaining a power balance between the Guilds and a network of spies to let him know what is going on. His best tool (the *Companion* says his biggest enemy) is Commander Vimes, who he can rely on to stir up the right kind of trouble when he wants it. And the man is so canny that it seems likely the temporary rule of Lord Rust in *Jingo* was a deliberate attempt to distance himself from a failure of foreign policy, allowing him to pull strings behind the scenes. After all, behind the scenes includes Leonard of Quirm, the great inventor.

The moments in the *Discworld* series when evil is really confronted are when characters emerge who are interested in power for power's sake, and are attracted by the trappings of power. Lord Rust in *Jingo* is one example of this, the modern vampire family in *Carpe Jugulum* is another. Of course it is difficult to have such characters appear in *Discworld* novels, since the mood is one of comedy, and for evil to be convincing there has to be the chance that the plot may switch to tragedy. Pratchett has walked this line closely whilst staying on the comedic side more often than any other writer I know.

A Note On This Book

Within these pages you will find commentaries on each of the books, from *The Carpet People* to *Thief Of Time*, plus briefer examinations of the maps and the companion. I've not had the space to deal with the plays – which are adaptations of the books after all – or the various cartoons. Personally I think that Pratchett is a writer who works best on paper.

Each entry includes details of first publication; aside from the special case of *The Carpet People*, later editions have not been tracked, although all of the current paperbacks are published by Corgi, part of Transworld. Collectors should note that there were New English Library editions of the first three novels prior to Corgi editions. American editions have proved too difficult to keep an eye on, since different publishers have brought out a number of books. Each book is given a location and a plot summary – where I am careful not to give away too many of the twists. I then give a listing of the major targets for humour – although targets implies too vicious a mood for most of the humour. The list is not meant to be exhaustive, since that would take up several books of this length. (Those with internet access might wish to look at the Annotated Pratchett Files – see the URL in the bibliography). I also note recurring characters – the wizards, the Librarian, witches, the City Watch, Death, Cohen, Greebo, Patrician Vetinari, CMOT Dibbler, and Gaspode – especially where that might not be obvious from the plot summary. Again this is not exhaustive – there are minor nobles, beggars and Casanunda who are recurring characters. Finally I discuss the themes of the novel – concentrating on any serious issues, occasionally criticising the novel – and give each one a mark out of five. The purpose of this last is clearly to annoy people – I'm not a big fan of the wizard novels, and this shows.

I'm firmly of the opinion that just because something is popular, it doesn't mean you can't analyse it. I've resisted the temptation simply to list funny bits – such is subjective anyway. And just because Pratchett writes comedies, doesn't mean his books don't deal with the real world. A consistent view of the world emerges from the books – but whether this is Pratchett's world-view I wouldn't want to say. I can only infer what Pratchett thinks; it's just my opinion. Whilst there are some places where I've risked a joke or an arcane reference of my own, I don't see the point (as a couple of reviewers have said of *Terry Pratchett: Guilty Of Literature*) of trying to compete with my subject who is wittier than I could ever be. Besides, if I do sound too serious, then just imagine this whole book as a parody of literary criticism...

Chapter One: The Early Novels

The Carpet People, The Dark Side Of The Sun, Strata.

The Carpet People

Published: Gerrards Cross: Colin Smythe, 1971; revised edition London: Gollancz, 1992.

Location: Between the east of the Carpet and Ware.

Story: The Munrung tribe, having wandered away from the centre of the empire for ten years, are stirred back into action by the destruction of their village. Rumours of the destructive forces of the Fray abound, as do tales of the evil mouls. Accompanied by the warrior Bane and then by Brocando, son of Broc, Lord of Jeopard, the Munrungs set out to defeat the mouls.

Major Targets: In some ways it's a fantasy dependent on *The Lord Of The Rings*; Snibril as a Frodo figure, shaman Pismire as Gandalf, Bane as Strider, cast out of their comfortable village or Shire towards the west, meeting wights on the way with bizarre powers and doing battle, hack and slash, with the mouls/orcs. Ish. Without all the songs, of course. And the Cracks of Doom. But it's clearly that kind of fantasy.

Subtext: The two main characters are brothers separated in age: the elder Glurk, the leader and warrior and figure of fun, and the younger Snibril, the thinker and the one who is brave because he faces down his fears. In any society based on merit, Snibril would be leader, except that he wouldn't want to be - a sensible decision that resonates through Pratchett's oeuvre.

Ware the capital is the centre of an empire, but with everything done that was needed to be done, it has stagnated. The emperors have shifted from being elected to being hereditary, and have fallen under the sway of unscrupulous advisors. Bane is particularly disgusted about this. Ware is here a stand-in for ancient Rome at the end of the empire.

The wights, with their ability to see the future, are worth attention; they seem very dispirited when they lose this power because how can they fight if they don't know the outcome? Culaina the thunorg, a character introduced in the revised edition, doesn't just remember what will happen, but what *might* happen. She can see all the possibilities of what could transpire. She is insistent that the smallest act can make a difference.

The point presumably is to fight if the outcome is worth the risk, and to try and avoid fighting if it isn't. Sensible trying is the point. For many, of course, war has become a game. Careus the sergeant is a crucial figure, who knows how to get the job of war done and who really runs things; higher ranks are just window dressing to give war some status. At the same time he doesn't make policy. Careus is given a job to fight: he does it.

The Verdict: There's some mileage in trying to work out the scale of the world and the nature of what they encounter (coins, hair, carpet thread, presumably dust mites and other microscopic creepy-crawlies), and the sentiments on democracy over kingship, especially in the second version, are worthy. It just doesn't hit too many funny bones. 2/5

The Dark Side Of The Sun

Published: Gerrards Cross: Colin Smythe, 1976.

Location: Widdershins and various other locations in the known universe.

Story: Dominickdaniel Sabalos, aka Dom, of Widdershins is heir to a great fortune. Indeed, he has a bank the size of a planet for a godfather and is fated to discover the lost world of the Jokers, an ancient hyperevolved species who have vanished from the known universe. Unfortunately, as Dom becomes Chairman of the Board, someone tries to assassinate him. He survives the attempt, in fact a number of attempts, and it seems unclear whether someone is trying to stop him from discovering Jokers World, or helping him to do so.

Major Targets: The Known Space novels of Larry Niven, the Foundation and Psychohistory plus the Laws of Robotics of Isaac Asimov (even a robot called Isaac) and any space opera populated with bizarre races of aliens – Ron Goulart, Jack Vance and Cordwainer Smith have all been mentioned by critics. There's a throwaway reference to *Henry IV Part II*. Is the title an echo of a Pink Floyd album?

Subtext: The Jokers are a super-evolved race who are the sort of beings that might build a Discworld, as a clue that something super-evolved has been wandering lazily by and just stopped for a little rest and recreation. Or creation, anyway. Indeed there are a couple of references that are picked up again in the *Discworld* series, notably a mention of Small Gods and a Hogswatchnight setting. The bank even speaks in capital letters, foreshadowing Death. For that matter Widdershins anticipates one of the directions on the Discworld.

What we have here is a rather rapid plot against a background of rabid invention – the various races including the phnobes and the drosks who are humanoid, and the Creapii, Tarquins and Spooners. The end result is somewhat breathless, and dense; and weighed further down with more information density by the presence of extracts from various speeches and documents. This is a ploy tried by a number of SF writers to flesh out their imagined universes; the model here is Isaac Asimov's *Foundation* sequence.

The *Foundation* sequence, or at least the first trilogy (1942-1950), is based around the idea of psychohistory, a mathematical way of predicting the generalised future, and around the establishment of two Foundations, one secret, to deal with the approaching collapse of the Empire and to shorten the period until civilisation is reborn. (One of Pratchett's species continually evolves and then willingly dismantles its civilisation in favour of barbarism.) Psychohistory failed to take into account the Mule, a mutant leader with paranormal powers who thus invalidated many of the predictions.

Here we have the Jokers Institute – dedicated to locating the lost Jokers and studying their artefacts – and the race of Jokers themselves. Just as the Second Foundation may not be at the other end of the galaxy but on the same planet as the First, so Jokers World may be outside of the universe altogether, or rather closer to home. The probability theory is melded together with ideas of quantum physics – which Pratchett returned to in the *Johnny Maxwell Trilogy*, especially *Johnny And The Bomb* – and the possibility of parallel universes, although not, yet, the Trousers Of Time. The probability equations seem to be blind to Dom.

The Verdict: Too manic for its own good. 1/5

Strata

Published: Gerrards Cross: Colin Smythe, 1981.

Location: Earth and then on a flat planet.

Story: Kin Arad is going about her everyday life designing and building planets when she is confronted by Jalo, who intrigues her about a planet he has found. A planet which is a flat disc. Kin and her colleagues Marco and Silver travel through space to this world, where they unfortunately crash into one of the orbiting planets and cannot take off again. As they explore the planet they've got three imperatives: to find out why the planet appears to be dying, to work out how to get back to Earth, and to do all this before Silver, who needs very specific proteins, gets hungry and has to eat something.

Major Targets: Larry Niven's *Ringworld* (1970) and *Ringworld Engineers* (1979). Roman, Viking and Arab history. In some ways the black monolith of Arthur C Clarke's *2001: A Space Odyssey* (1968).

Cameos: Death. Believe it or not, yes, but only very briefly, and not quite the same character we've grown to love. For that matter there's a mention of a tavern called the Broken Drum, later known as the central inn to the city of Ankh-Morpork.

Subtext: Imagine a science fiction comedy which involves people who build planets. Try *The Hitchhiker's Guide To The Galaxy* (radio series 1978, in particular episodes three and four; book 1979), by Douglas Adams, in which the Earth is revealed to be a giant computer manufactured by the Magratheans for a race of hyperintelligent mice. There's a quote which appears on some of the *Discworld* novels about how Adams would have never had the success he had if Pratchett had come along first. Well, he did, and he did anyway. Given the length of time Pratchett must have spent writing the novel, who got there first? Of course, the idea of planet building was not new to Adams (and Pratchett had explored it to some extent in *The Dark Side Of The Sun*). Robert Sheckley's novel *Dimension Of Miracles* (1968) features planet builders, and the line 'And be sure you're wearing gloves [when you handle the sun]! That thing's hot!' No doubt there are other examples.

Nor is the idea of a flat planet new to Pratchett; a number of religions and philosophers such as Ptolemy got there first. In fact this is a Ptolemaic planet, the centre of the universe for anyone inhabiting it, and complete with planets which have to reverse orbits to appear to regress properly. All that's missing is a soundtrack of the music of the spheres.

The *Discworld* series is not the only work that it looks forward to; there are also anticipations of the alternate histories which emerge in *Johnny And The Bomb*, although without the Trousers Of Time. In Kin's world Rome was named after Remus rather than his twin Romulus, but on this artificial world the reverse is true. Here the Vikings have explored America much more thoroughly than our histories allow. And the Arabs are much closer to *The Thousand And One Nights*.

Just as the book looks forward, it also looks back. *The Dark Side Of The Sun* featured the search for Jokers World, the home of a vanished race who have left their mighty works behind. Here Earth is obsessed with the Spindles, who have done much the same. The Discworld seems to be another piece of evidence for a vanished race, perhaps even mightier than the Spindles. The twist in this is very cleverly set up. Kin has to watch for her engineers getting bored and laying down anachronistic objects in the strata of the planets they are manufacturing. The wrong object in the wrong place could completely throw an evolving race. This is no mere comic detail, but a carefully established foreshadowing of how the book turns out.

Meanwhile there is a planet which looks and feels like a fantasy landscape, complete with demons, djinns and flying carpets, but which turns out to have a perfectly lucid scientific explanation. Here the black and white of rationality wins out over the colour of magic, in a way that they never will again in Pratchett's novels. We don't know where the Discworld comes from, other than it seems to be held together with the magic of consensus belief, a belief which, if it fades, can have cosmic consequences (see *Hogfather*, say). Here though the world is constructed to fulfil a whole set of beliefs.

The Verdict: Getting there; a dry run for a lot of what is going to happen in the *Discworld* series, but with a veneer of scientific plausibility. 3/5

Chapter Two: Discworld

From *The Colour Of Magic* to *Thief Of Time*.

The Colour Of Magic

Published: Gerrards Cross: Colin Smythe, 1983.

Setting: Between Ankh-Morpork and the hub.

Story: Rincewind, an inept wizard, is blackmailed into acting as a guide for Twoflower, a tourist from Bes Palargic. Twoflower is keen to see all the sights of Ankh-Morpork – and is particularly pleased to witness a pub brawl in the Broken Drum. He later causes the pub – and much of the city – to be burnt down for the insurance money. Outside of the city, Rincewind and Twoflower find themselves in a temple, a lair where dragons exist if you believe in them, and finally, after many adventures, end up on the rim of the Disc, as sacrifices.

Major Targets: The fantasy genre is the target here, with twists on the various tropes of such writing. The highwaymen Bravd and Weasel owe a debt of names to Fritz Lieber's characters Fafhrd and the Gray Mouser (the place name Lankhmar also gives us Ankh-Morpork). Hrun the Barbarian is a variation on Robert E Howard's Conan. Twoflower's character is established as a Japanese tourist, eager to have photographs (or, rather, paintings) of everything he sees. An offer of something to suck whilst on a dragon suggests the rather mundane reality of being on an aeroplane (one of which also appears briefly).

Cameos: Death: The first mention of Death – as having a sense of humour – occurs in a reference to a soothsayer who sees the coming fire and rides away, only to die in a mud slide. Death shows up every few pages, since he deals personally with dying wizards, and Rincewind is at risk a great deal. We see Death's garden, meet his white horse, and learn he has many servants. *The Librarian:* Mentioned as too busy to look after the Octavo, the magic book containing the eight most powerful spells. *The Watch:* They show up at the Broken Drum, but are careful not to intervene too soon. *Wizards:* Aside from Rincewind, we never see them here. There is a female wizard later on, but she is presumably not attached to Unseen University. *The Patrician:* Here unnamed, with a network of spies, he ensures that Rincewind does his duty. Or else. *Unseen University:* Rincewind studied and failed there, and we discover it has a faculty of Minor Religions.

Subtext: A standard narrative strategy of utopian fiction is showing a visitor around the land, and whilst this utopia is closer to no-place than good-place, the tour shapes this book. Twoflower speaks a different language from the denizens of Ankh-Morpork, and his naïveté means that he is in severe danger of being robbed of the hundreds of gold coins he is carrying, as well as being likely to wander into places best avoided. We can presume he is a speedy learner, since his phrase book is forgotten about after the first chapter.

Yes, chapter. Unusually for Pratchett, this book is divided into four distinct chapters: 'The Colour Of Magic' (which is Octarine, the eighth colour of the rainbow), 'The Sending Of Eight' (wizards are superstitious about... the number between seven and nine), 'The Lure Of The Wyrm' (a Bram Stoker reference – compare *The Lair Of The White Worm*) and 'Close To The Edge' (an album by Yes, with Roger Dean artwork that is reminiscent of the Discworld itself, but minus elephants and a turtle). In these stories we go from Ankh-Morpork (presumably halfway between the hub and the rim) to the rim, and beyond, as Rincewind goes over the edge at the end. There is even mention of the Counter-Weight continent, setting a scene for books nearly two decades later.

The narrative resembles a cookie dough cutter: danger, escape, danger, escape, as Rincewind finds himself in a crisis and has to extricate himself with little more than his wits – and that may be very little indeed. Hot on their heels is Luggage, a trunk made of sapient pearwood and with hundreds of little legs, loyal to Twoflower even in the most extreme circumstances. That Twoflower is condemned to death part-way through the book seems to have been forgotten about, but here logic is not as important as comic effect: at one point Rincewind falls through the dimensions to end up on a TWA aeroplane, at the risk of shattering the fantasy frame in search of a joke.

The Verdict: Sets the scene for the sequence, but a little limited. 2/5

The Light Fantastic

Published: Gerrards Cross: Colin Smythe, 1986.

Location: Between the hub and Ankh-Morpork.

Story: Rincewind, last seen falling off the edge of the world, is rescued, along with the spell which is lodged in his memory. Meanwhile the wizards summon Death, who warns them that unless the eight spells are said at a certain point, the world will end. Rincewind's presence is clearly required and Trymon, a wizard on the rise, will stop at nothing to get him. Rincewind, Twoflower and the Luggage wander from one crisis to another, aided by Cohen the Barbarian, blissfully unaware of quite what is going on, and how they've emerged unscathed so far.

Major Targets: Again epic fantasy, with Robert E Howard's Conan depicted as an old man, and the horse clans from *Lord Of The Rings*. The wizards rather resemble the schoolmasters from Mervyn Peake's *Gormenghast* (1950), with Trymon as the Machiavellian Steerpike. The appearance of a gingerbread cottage introduces a riff on witches and fairy tales, and mentions of tooth fairies and Hogswatchnight prepare the ground for later books in the series.

Cameos: Death: Firstly summoned by the wizards, then visits a dying wizard and is visited by Rincewind. He has a daughter, Ysabell, and is rather confusingly called Mort (see *Mort*). He is taught a game we can infer is bridge, which is an alternative to chess and allows more people to play at once (keeping War, Pestilence and Famine occupied, which can't be a bad thing). *The Librarian:* Here turned into an orangutan by an errant spell, and can be bribed with bananas. We learn something of L-Space, in that the magic of the books distorts the dimensions of the library. *Witches:* Offstage, or rather away from the cottage. Witches are female and wizards are male, and witches can't go to the Unseen University because of deficits in the plumbing. *Wizards:* Inept, and surviving despite rather than because of their actions. Whilst they are no doubt ambitious and backbiting, they are also set in their ways. *Cohen:* His first appearance, lisping his way through life because of rotten teeth. He does acquire a spare set though. *Unseen University:* There is a Dean of Liberal Studies, but the wizards with their orders are the focus of attention here.

Subtext: Straightforwardly and obviously a sequel, which sheds the tourist itinerary in favour of finding one's way home, a route which passes talking trees, toadstools inhabited by gnomes, trolls and flying rocks headed for the Discworld equivalent of Stonehenge. The fantasy illusion is shattered here and there by references to countries or people on Earth; whilst the wizards are meant to evoke the dons of Oxbridge in the popular imagination – from before Peake to after David Lodge – a clear reference to, say, *Nice Work* would bring too much reality into it. Reality, however, impinges into a running joke on the accuracy of literary descriptions; what, for example, should a face that launched a thousand ships look like? Pratchett gives us two examples, whereas one, or three, would be funnier. Here he begins to get to grips with the idea of narrative (and the thought that inevitably there is a narrator), an idea to which he returns throughout the series.

The Verdict: Aside from Bethany, a horsewoman, this is an almost exclusively male world, which sets the scene for a feminist/feminine backlash in the next book. Although better structured as a book than *The Colour Of Magic*, I can't help but feel that Rincewind is rather too obviously a comic character who seems to have two modes: panic and sheer bloody panic. 3/5

Equal Rites

Published: London: Gollancz in association with Colin Smythe Ltd, 1987.

Location: Bad Ass, in the Ramtops Mountains, thence to Ankh-Morpork and Unseen University.

Story: Drum Billet is dying and goes in search of his successor wizard, finding the infant Esk. Rather than being the eighth son of an eighth son, Esk is the daughter (with seven brothers) of an eighth son. Which rather buggers up being a wizard. She is taken in hand by the witch Granny Weatherwax, and begins to learn some magic, but the lure of the Lore is too much, and Esk sets out to become a wizard.

Major Targets: The institutional sexism of some (male) establishments, such as (formerly) Oxbridge and the church. Some of our notions about witches are also played with; Weatherwax has a grasp on psychology (headology) and life experience and also conducts magic. Unseen University is explicitly compared to Gormenghast, architecturally speaking.

Cameos: Death: Comes to collect Drum Billet's soul, as is his right. *The Librarian:* Esk starts cleaning the Library and the Librarian remains as an orangutan. He is somewhat upset when, thanks to Esk's throwing of her wizard's staff into the Ankh, the library is flooded. *Witches:* This is the first appearance of Granny Weatherwax, one of Pratchett's most complex and satisfyingly developed characters – who might possibly be related to a wizard of the same surname. Whilst Granny Weatherwax knew Nanny Annaple as a child, and meets Hilda on her travels, she is a witch who operates alone. At the start of the novel she is a midwife, a traditional wise woman rôle. Witches, we learn, are all female and draw their powers from the earth, whereas... *Wizards:* Are all male (until Esk, oh, and the female one in *The Colour Of Magic*) and draw their powers from the sky. They are a lazy, ineffectual, sexist lot. *Unseen University:* Here it seems to be synonymous with the wizards, and faculty seems identical to university. Clearly Pratchett is not *au fait* with the ins and outs of university politics, but that's something in his favour.

Subtext: The title gives some indication of the theme: Wizards are all male, and this is entirely natural and stands to reason. And witches are female and a male witch is a contradiction in terms – he'd be a warlock. On the other hand, this seems all a matter of semantics and the difference in theory is merely the source of the magic (although in practice this barely matters and Weatherwax can hold her own against the Archchancellor). If the admission of women to a university is simply a matter of a problem with plumbing, then sort out the plumbing. Tradition here seems to be a bit of a dead weight. Both Esk and Weatherwax have great powers – of survival as they wander through strange lands, of persuasion as they try to continue their journeys and finally of magic as they face the inertia of things being done because that's the way things have always been done. Pratchett's feminism never becomes strident, and seems impossible to dispute; this novel was even serialised on BBC Radio 4's *Woman's Hour*.

The Verdict: The best of the sequence so far, which isn't too hard given it's the third. Rincewind does not appear, which is a good thing, and it's refreshing to have a female protagonist – in fact, two. 4/5

Mort

Published: London: Gollancz in association with Colin Smythe Ltd, 1987.

Location: A village in the Ramtops, Death's Domain, Sto Lat, Ankh-Morpork and other locations.

Story: Mort, the youngest son of a farming family, is apprenticed to Death. He begins to learn the trade, but his master is often absent (Death has decided to discover what it is like to be human). Rather than taking the Princess Keli's soul at her death, Mort kills her assassin and saves her life. Unfortunately as a result of her not dying, the predestined unification of the cities of Sto Lat and Sto Helit will not happen, and a new reality is created. Mort has to keep on top of the job and ensure reality gets back to more or less where it should be.

Major Targets: Our ideas of death (*Death Takes A Holiday* (1934) and *The Seventh Seal* (1956)) and also about the conditions and experience of working (and getting a job). Death becomes a job – he goes out on his rounds, like a milkman – and when Death wants a new occupation, he finds it hard to find work as an experienced scythe-wielder.

Cameos: Death: Well, obviously, as this is the first of the novels to focus on Death. He is no longer called Mort, can't remember Mort's name, has an adopted daughter named Ysabell, a servant called Albert (a reference to *Batman*?) and a horse called Binky. And he's kind to kittens. *The Librarian:* Seen briefly in Unseen University and involved in the Rite of AshkEnte; Rincewind is assistant librarian. *The Watch:* Glimpsed briefly guarding gates to cities. *Witches:* One of the first souls that Mort takes is that of a witch and she is very understanding about his inexperience. *Wizards*: Mort is mistaken for a wizard because he walks through a wall. Wizards are also entitled to be collected by Death. After not dying, Keli visits the twenty-year-old Igneous Cutwell and appoints him as Royal Recogniser. Later on the Unseen University wizards are seen and get involved in the Rite to bind

Death. *The Patrician:* Mort is sold the Patrician's horse. *Unseen University:* Founded by Alberto Malich, who two thousand years ago became Death's manservant.

Subtext: Death becomes a very human character; humanity is the animal that works and there is no escape from work for Death, or any time off in lieu. He is not cruel and doesn't see himself as bringing justice, just a release from the current life. But there is no escaping the dust of aeons that hangs over Death's Domain; Ysabell has been stuck at the age of sixteen since she was rescued by Death and it might have been kinder to let her die. (Princess Keli's death, whilst at an early age, would have led to a period of peace and prosperity; death is not something to be afraid of or something evil, but a natural process which may have positive consequences for those left behind.) Mort as his apprentice mirrors many of Death's attributes: both are naïve and yet can withstand the machinations of conmen, both can hold their liquor and both have difficulties in dealing with women.

People seem to get the afterlife they believe in – even if that means reincarnation. There is indeed a very strong sense that people can make their own fate by their own decisions and actions, despite the fact that each person's life seems to be written down in a book. The impact of belief is in fact one which powers much of the workings of the *Discworld* series, whether it is dragons that need to be believed in, headology, self-identity or as readers recognising what we think we know about a particular subject. With those beliefs, especially a belief in the self, in mind, the individual has to go out and live. Mort and Ysabell both choose mortality in an attempt to change the world rather than living a quiet detached life. Death, in contrast, has to return to his duty and to dealing in death because, paradoxically, it is the only life for him.

It's also worth noting that, after the feminism of *Equal Rites*, we have two more strong female characters, Ysabell and Keli. Ysabell, in working on the nodes which bind the fabric of the universe together (one of Death's jobs), is clear that Mort and Albert are helping her, not the other way round. On the other hand, the book is about Mort and Death, and not about her.

The Verdict: Another step forward, with the most tightly and satisfyingly constructed of the novels to date. Pratchett plays with our idea of the medieval conception of Death and contemporary working practices. 5/5

Sourcery

Published: London: Gollancz in association with Colin Smythe Ltd, 1988.

Location: A village, Ankh-Morpork and Klatch, among other places.

Story: Ipslore, an eighth son of an eighth son and much against the practices of wizards, is a wizard and has married and had eight sons. As Death comes to collect him, he disappears into a metal wizard's staff and vows to use his son to gain power in Ankh-Morpork and beyond. As the son, Coin, takes over Unseen University, so the Archchancellor's hat decides to make a break for it, taking Rincewind along with him.

Major Targets: Practices of magic and management by committee, Arab culture as perceived through Coleridge or Omar Kayyam and the end of the world.

Cameos: Death: Comes to collect a wizard's soul. Twice. And Death's mates, Pestilence, Famine and War are along for the ride. Only they've just popped into the pub for a swift half. *The Librarian:* Still looking after the books with Rincewind as his assistant. *Wizards:* Another crowd, another Archchancellor, and rather bamboozled by Coin's powers and ideas. *Cohen:* Or rather his daughter, Cohina. *The Patrician:* Now Vetinari (or finally given a name), with a lethal spy network, vanquished by Coin. *Unseen University:* Pretty well destroyed by the actions of the book. Or rather actions of characters, which is to say people within the book, so as not to confuse this with books within the Discworld, which are pretty damn powerful.

Subtext: The wizards have great power, through their use of magic, and could set themselves up as rulers if they so wished. Fortunately, laziness, infighting and a Byzantine power structure – with a pyramid of power based on the number eight – mean that they are too concerned with their own affairs, the next meal and possible promotion. Coin threatens all this, with his abilities as a sourceror, that is to create new magic without the need for spells. Such magic threatens first the stability of Ankh-Morpork (not that it is particularly stable at the best of times, but as hopelessly chaotic anarchies go, it does at least function) and then even the nature of the Discworld itself. In *The Light Fantastic* the Discworld risked striking a star, and *Mort's* actions in *Mort* meant that possibilities were flapping around loose, but here the danger is so much more apocalyptic hence the need for Famine, Pestilence and War, as well as Death. Power corrupts, and it's not clever.

The Verdict: Last time it was magic that brought Rincewind back to Ankh-Morpork, this time he's sent away. I'm not really a fan of the Rincewind books. Could you tell? 3/5

Wyrd Sisters

Published: London: Gollancz, 1988. An extract appeared in *Interzone* 26 (November/December 1988) prior to book publication.

Location: The kingdom of Lancre, around the Ramtops Mountains and briefly in Ankh-Morpork.

Story: The king of Lancre, Verence, is murdered by his cousin Lord Leonal Felmet and begins to haunt the castle. His son and crown fall into the hands of three witches, Granny Weatherwax, Nanny Ogg and Magrat, who have come together to form a coven. They foster the child with a travelling theatre troupe. Meanwhile Lord Felmet is becoming increasingly paranoid about being exposed and is suspicious of witches - he plots to have them discredited. The three witches, wary of getting involved in politics, realise they have to bring the lost heir back, but it would be fifteen years before he could be a viable monarch... Time for magic, then.

Major Targets: Clearly the wife and husband murdering team, with the husband being increasingly wracked with guilt, is a version of *Macbeth*, particularly when the three witches are taken into account. The ghost and the rôle of a play in displaying a guilty murderer are lifted from *Hamlet* (which lifted its narrative in turn from earlier plays by Thomas Kyd, *The Spanish Tragedy* and a lost version of *Hamlet*). Meanwhile the theatre troupe's resident playwright, Hwel, is a version of the Immortal Bard and writes speeches that could fit in *Henry V*, *Henry IV Part Two* and *As You Like It*. Hwel, one of those characters in the Discworld who gets struck by ideas, is working on clowns who bear uncanny resemblances to Charlie Chaplin, the Marx Brothers and Laurel and Hardy. And some of the witches' conversations recall fairy stories – *Cinderella*, *Hansel And Gretel* and *Sleeping Beauty*.

Cameos: Death: Initially to let King Verence know he is going to be haunting the castle and later as a walk-on in the play. *The Librarian:* Very briefly in a tavern and then in a tavern brawl. *Witches:* Esk is not mentioned, but the young witch Magrat has brought Granny Weatherwax and Nanny Ogg together for a coven. Witches, like wizards, are not the marrying kind, but given Nanny Ogg's vast family (and increasing number of descendants) she has, er, bred. She has a reputation, naturally, for being promiscuous, but only Granny Weatherwax dare say this to her face. (We later learn she has had three marriages officially, although in these rural areas the practice itself is somewhat informal.) There is mention here of Black Aliss, a witch who presumably went to the bad and was killed in her own oven, and is seen as a salutary example to the witches about using their magic. *Wizards:* Only mentioned in contrast to witches: wizards like hierarchies, witches like more anarchistic arrangements. *Greebo*: Nanny Ogg's cat first appears, lured into the castle (somehow) by Verence to try and get Ogg to follow, which she does. The Fool, bravely and foolishly, rescues Greebo from a career as a castle mouser and a lifetime of beds for sleeping on and tapestries for climbing and urinating on. *Patrician Vetinari:* His policies of licensing crime are described. *Vampires:* Lancre had a vampire Queen Grimnir the Impaler.

Subtext: Pratchett reintroduces Granny Weatherwax from *Equal Rites* and gives her companions to spark off and spar with: the traditional three witches of *Macbeth* and three weird sisters of myth. The reality, this being comedy, doesn't quite match up and the two older witches aren't certain they want to be tied down to a coven. And the traditional magic ways are reinterpreted through their not having the right equipment and having to improvise; as well as Magrat's vegetarian ethics.

The novel offers a commentary on power, as begun in *Sourcery*. The two older witches have power which they fear to use; Magrat's power is coming along but is just out of her control. Lord Felmet is an abuser of power and it is clear that he is shaping up to be a tyrant if he is allowed to rule – but to usurp him could be just as dangerous. (Remember *Mort*, where the saving of the innocent Princess Keli might have prevented the better long-term aim of uniting Sto Lat and Sto Herit.) The Fool, thinking he is doing the right thing, persuades Felmet to use the power of words rather than arms, and the spread of rumour is a form of headology. Tomjon, the rightful heir to the throne, is much more interested in acting as King in plays than in being a King in real life.

Of course, a power vacuum would be worse and a candidate is found in true carnivalesque fashion; the attentive reader should have been expecting this all along.

The Verdict: Utterly splendid. 5/5

Pyramids

(The Book Of Going Forth)

Published: London: Gollancz, 1989. An extract appeared in *Gaslight And Ghosts*, eds. Stephen Jones and Jo Fletcher, 1988 World Fantasy Convention, London, and Robinson Publishing, in 1988, prior to book publication.

Location: Ankh-Morpork, Djelibeybi and the borders with other kingdoms.

Story: Teppic, heir to the throne of Djelibeybi, is learning to be an assassin whilst waiting to assume his rightful place. But his father dies and he is called to his duties – which are many and onerous, although real power lies with Dios the priest. The crisis comes when he intervenes in the execution of a handmaid. Meanwhile Dios has ordered the building of a pyramid as a monument to Teppic's father, a pyramid that is simply too damn big to be safe, either economically or magically.

Major Targets: Egypt (or what we think we know about it), duties of heirs (think of Teppic as Prince Charles), driving tests, and Greek mythology.

Cameos: Death: To collect the soul of Teppicymon XXVII. *The Watch:* Mentioned in passing in Ankh-Morpork, and there's a Djelibeybi equivalent.

Subtext: In memory, *Pyramids* seems hardly to be a *Discworld* novel at all. The setting is the kingdom of Djelibeybi, an analogue for Egypt stuffed full of all the Egyptological details you thought you'd remembered from school. Death and the Librarian play no more than cameo roles, if indeed the Librarian appears at all. As the ongoing series stretched its legs, Pratchett seemed to be desperately seeking for models beyond SF and fantasy to parody. The pun Djelibeybi seems weak and pointless, and there are further cringe-making examples.

Stylistically it is like the other novels, with the cinematic zooming-in description of space and the Discworld, poised on the back of four elephants on top of the great tortoise A'Tuin. Then there are the flaring pyramids, whose light may 'in chapters to come, illuminate many mysteries . . . It will certainly show what our ancestors would be thinking if they were alive today.' Like the other books in the sequence, it is not divided into chapters, although unusually it is divided into individual books. There are the footnotes, as always, Pratchett's evolution of the stand-up comedian's control of timing. Indeed, timing is more important in this novel than the others.

It appears to be seats-of-pants-plotting, but it must be carefully structured, as a doubled narrative of Teppic learning to be an assassin and being examined foreshadows the chaos to follow. Everyone knows the myth about how razor blades keep a sharp edge when stored under pyramids, and if this is really true then there must be some sort of time dilation going on – it is fixed in time at the point of being sharp. When a particularly large pyramid is built toward the end of the book, then the time dilation effects threaten to rupture reality. All the dead kings of the kingdom are resurrected from their pyramidic tombs; the line about knowing what ancestors will think of modern civilisation turns out in fact to have been a prediction.

What is perhaps more threatening for the rest of the Discworld is that the two countries Tsort and Ephebe (Pratchett's version of classical Greece) become neighbours with the disappearance of the old kingdom of Djelibeybi. At this point territorial aggression overspills – thanks to 'Historical imperative', according to one Ephebian philosopher – giving a chance for a comic rerun of the Trojan Wars, complete with Trojan Horse (in fact a herd of Trojan Horses). There is a risk in dealing with war in a comic novel, although both Joseph Heller and Kurt Vonnegut have pulled off this feat in the past. Death certainly occurs in the *Discworld* novels, on occasion in a rather grim manner. But on this occasion the action stops just short of the predicted massacre. The return of time intervenes, just in time. It would be folly to give away the ending, save to note that it has to do with time, which can be cyclical; the snake eating its own tail having become a motif in the text.

Coo: Pyramids is the only novel by Pratchett to date to have won the BSFA Award.

The Verdict: The most fiendishly constructed of the novels to date, yielding new pleasures on each successive rereading. 4/5 But as a *Discworld* novel, 2/5

Guards! Guards!

Published: London: Gollancz, 1989.

Location: Briefly in a community of dwarfs, but mostly in Ankh-Morpork.

Story: Carrot, a human adopted by dwarfs, is sent by his family to work in the City Watch of Ankh-Morpork. Meanwhile a secret brotherhood is threatening the city by summoning up a dragon and aiming to remove the Patrician from power in favour of someone they can control. Captain Samuel Vimes, the drunken head of the City Watch, begins to investigate a number of deaths by fire and concludes a dragon is at large. Can he track it down before any more people die or Ankh-Morpork falls into the hands of other powers?

Major Targets: Detective and noir fiction and films, with shades of Humphrey Bogart, the disposable characters in stories like *Star Trek*, narratives about folk tales of dragons (with shades of *The Hobbit*) and Barbara Woodhouse, the dog trainer who became a TV star in the early 1980s.

Cameos: Death: Comes to collect a couple of victims. *The Librarian:* His largest rôle to date, beginning with his discovery of the theft of a book, *The Summoning Of Dragons*, and his induction into the City Watch. *The Watch:* Led by Captain Vimes, with Nobby, Colon and Carrot among his men. *Witches:* Mistress Garlick (Magrat?) is mentioned early on. *Wizards:* The Elucidated Brethren of the Ebon Night can do magic, but the only other appearance of anything wizard-like is the Archchancellor at a council of war. *Patrician Vetinari:* Imprisoned during the course of the novel, although it's never entirely clear whether this isn't part of his plans – he has an impressive speech about the nature of humanity and evil. *Unseen University:* We visit the library and L-Space within it. *Cut-My-Own-Throat (CMOT) Dibbler:* His first appearance, selling goods to the crowds.

Subtext: At the start of *Guards! Guards!*, Pratchett includes a dedication to the guards and security officers who act as extras in all kind of narratives, and who are canon fodder to the actions of the hero and villain. The one in the red jumper in *Star Trek* (aside from Scotty, natch) is always going to get it. In Carrot, Nobby, Colon and (briefly) Gaskin such characters are put centre stage and we are meant to care about them. Gaskin is killed off pretty quickly, before we've really learnt to empathise with him, but there are moments when we really wonder about their safety. The comic impulse (which paradoxically makes it harder to care) actually protects them, particularly in a series of million to one chances. We do certainly care about these characters, but at this point Pratchett isn't quite assured enough to kill off a major character (this will come later).

Carrot, with his mysterious origins and meaningful sword, it seems that he is being set up with the same kind of inheritance as Tomjon from *Wyrd Sisters*. (For a place that has not had kings for three hundred years, Ankh-Morpork seems to be acquiring lost heirs at an alarming rate.) This is a narrative to which Pratchett will return. Meanwhile, Carrot shows up the rest of the Watch with his detailed knowledge of city ordinances and the dangerous activity of trying to arrest the licensed thieves and assassins of the city. This perhaps shames Vimes into action, the clichéd drunken cop, drinking to forget... well, it's not entirely clear what, and he's probably forgotten. He can sober up to save the day, and may well end up clean living if his budding relationship with dragon trainer Lady Ramkin goes anywhere serious.

Alongside Vimes' alcoholism there is a sense of the series growing up. There is probably more swearing in this novel than the preceding volumes put together; this is intriguing in that, although Pratchett isn't here a children's writer, he does have many young readers in his audience. It's also worth noting the increased level of innuendo; Vimes and Lady Sybil's developing relationship, love between dragons, but most importantly Carrot's lodgings is a brothel. Sexuality had more or less been glossed over before (aside from Albert and Mort's father talking to Mort), but here the joke is more sustained. Vimes, drunkenly, mutters that the city is a woman, and his woman is Lady Ramkin. Ankh-Morpork is a city that has been under siege and historically what happens is that the invaders enter and merge into the population. In a revision of Vimes' metaphor, he is besieged by Lady

Ramkin, and has to conquer her; sooner or later he must merge with her. And that, of course, will have consequences for his whole identity.

The Verdict: The start of a new *Discworld* sequence, the City Watch, and a very rich novel. 4/5

~~Faust~~ Eric

Note: Presumably because it was originally published by Gollancz in hardback and paperback edition, this is not included in the numbering of the Corgi editions of the *Discworld* novels (which stopped numbering with *Moving Pictures* as number nine). *The Truth* is number twenty-five, including *Eric*, not twenty-four.

Published: London: Gollancz, 1990; originally published with Josh Kirby illustrations. In fact Josh Kirby got equal billing with Pratchett.

Location: Death's Domain, Ankh-Morpork, Pseudopolis and a number of other locations, past, present and future.

Story: Unseen University is haunted – possibly by Rincewind, as the wizards discover when they summon Death. Meanwhile Eric, a young boy, summons Rincewind and, mistaking him for a demon, demands three wishes. Reluctantly, Rincewind tries to grant them.

Major Targets: Greek mythology – the Trojan Wars, complete with horse – and the Faust(us) story.

Cameos: Death: Summoned by the Wizards. *The Librarian:* Appears briefly early on. *Wizards:* Complete with new Archchancellor, and they summon Death. *Unseen University:* Haunted by something. *Vampires:* Rincewind considers if he is one.

Subtext: A slender volume and a slender tale written at the height of Pratchett's productivity, half the length of *Guard! Guards!* or *Moving Pictures*. Is this aimed at children? Children whose parents don't mind the oshitoshitoshit cry towards the start presumably.

Rincewind's back, having wandered in the Dungeon Dimensions since *Sourcery*, and the Luggage is just behind him. Rincewind remembers the eight spells, but doesn't think about how he was possessed by one of them. OK, it's something you would want to forget, but would you manage to? Sometimes there's a feeling as if he's a different Rincewind, just as sometimes it appears to be a different Discworld.

Actually there *is* a different Rincewind, or rather a distant ancestor, who is an equivalent of Ulysses or Odysseus from *The Odyssey* and *The Iliad*. The Discworld Helen of Troy analogue had been mentioned before, especially in relation to what a face would look like having been used to launch ships with, and again the myth is undercut. The reader of this book needs at least a passing knowledge of the tales of Troy.

The Verdict: Not good. There are a couple of fun set pieces, but some of the humour is just too Earth-orientated, and Eric is woefully undeveloped. 1/5

Moving Pictures

Published: London: Gollancz, 1990.

Location: Ankh-Morpork and Holy Wood.

Story: A magical material is discovered which imps can paint pictures on, and which can in turn be projected onto screens by careful use of a salamander. Young Victor, studying to be a wizard at Unseen University, is drawn to the industry which is springing up in Holy Wood, as is Cut-My-Own-Throat Dibbler, who knows the opportunity to sell a sausage in a bun when he sees one. As Dibbler transforms an educational tool into spectacle, the staff and students of Unseen University find themselves transfixed by these moving pictures. Can Gaspode the Wonder Dog save them all?

Major Targets: Hollywood in general – Fred Astaire's audition, *Blues Brothers, Gone With The Wind*, Disney cartoons, *Lassie, The Wizard Of Oz, King Kong, Casablanca, Attack Of The 50 Foot Woman...*

Cameos: Death: Collects soul of the gatekeeper and returns at the climactic show. *The Librarian:* Quite a fan of moving pictures, and often to be found in the stalls, munching peanuts. Something must disturb him, because he goes to do some research about coming attractions in the dread volume *Necrotelicomnicon*. Later on he is to be found swinging from a vine through the city. And at this point he becomes an orang-utan, not an orangutan. *The Watch:* A couple of brief cameos for the officers, commenting on the action rather than acting. Detritus, the troll, is here one of Dibbler's employees, but he'll be back. *Witches:* No witches, but a couple of broomsticks. *Wizards:* We briefly see wizard training (half a decade before Harry Potter) and then the actions of the wizards when they learn of sinister events unfolding. *Cohen:* He is featured in a moving picture. *Patrician Vetinari:* Mentioned a couple of times, but then glimpsed at the première of *Blown Away*, eclipsed by Victor and Ginger, the stars of the film. *Unseen University:* Here there is another new Archchancellor, Ridcully. Ponder Stibbons appears, and so forth. The personnel of the University more or less settles down at this point. *CMOT Dibbler:* He moves from sausage-in-a-bun merchant to Holy Wood producer in one easy bound, with all the sensibilities of a Discworld Samuel Goldwyn. *Gaspode:* His first heroic appearance.

Subtext: A new medium is discovered that could change the world, and chaos ensues. This is something that will happen in *Soul Music*. The trick at this point is to be able to spot the originals that Pratchett is gently spoofing; the Librarian's screenplay of an ape abandoned in a city, growing up with humans, is of course an inversion of *Tarzan*. And by the end of the novel, the Librarian is swinging through the city. He then collides with a female figure escaped from a film, some fifty foot tall. So, *Attack Of The 50 Foot Woman*. Except that an ape and a woman together gives the opportunity for a *King Kong* riff. Aeroplanes are going to be difficult to manage though.

Sometimes Pratchett tips his hand too much by directly naming Earth characters, but not here; he leaves it to us to find the comparisons. There are plenty of elephants, but Cecil B DeMille's name does not pass his word processor. Mercifully he allows the film buff or cinephile to get the joke, and if the allusion is missed, then there are enough others to give most people a grin of recognition.

Ideas constantly seem to leak into the Discworld, and presumably there are only a limited number of crazes that are sufficiently world-changing for Pratchett to use; rock music in *Soul Music* and the printed word in *The Truth*. Perhaps computers will be the next topic to come up.

The Verdict: Great fun if you know your Hollywood. Or anyone else's, for that matter. 4/5

Reaper Man

Published: London: Gollancz, 1991.

Location: Death's Domain, a village in the Ramtops near Sheepridge and Ankh-Morpork.

Story: Death is made redundant because of the way he has been acting human, but he is allowed to keep Binky the horse. Meanwhile the wizard Windle Poons is looking forward to his death, indeed enjoys it, but rather embarrassingly sticks around. And he is joined by increasing numbers of the not dead.

Major Targets: Rural ritual, employment practices, the undead.

Cameos: Death: A major character who, having been sacked, finds work on a farm, scything. *The Librarian:* Back in his library, refusing to let some people in on the grounds that they are dead. And spelt orangutan. *The Watch:* Colon appears and witnesses one of Poons' suicide attempts. He has a couple more appearances, and the day Watch is mentioned. *Witches:* Specifically excluded for some reason by Death from helping in a domestic crisis (presumably because they'll recognise him?). *Wizards:* Especially Windle Poons. *Patrician Vetinari:* A brief appearance or two. *Unseen Uni-*

versity: In the new cast as introduced in the previous novel. *Vampires:* These are among the undead met by Windle. *CMOT Dibbler:* He's here again, bemused by the glass balls that are materialising in his store; still he knows a marketing opportunity when he sees one.

Subtext: Towards the end of *Moving Pictures*, when a non-human character is apparently dying, Death tells them that he is all there is, that he is Death to all... well, presumably excluding himself. In the course of the restructuring that goes on during *Reaper Man*, there emerges a Death of Rats.

Actually, Death is usually outside of time, but as a price for wishing to understand how mortals live (as opposed to being there when they die) he is punished by whatever powers that be (or are) by being sacked and made mortal. Of course, there aren't many openings for people of a certain age who have scythe-wielding skills, which is why he ends up working on exactly the kind of farm which he took Mort away from. During his sojourn there he becomes even more human in his dealings with the householder, Miss Flitworth, a character with a tragic history of her own. Then comes a crisis: he, a being with but few years to live, is given the chance to rescue someone who should have many years ahead of them. At first his response is similar to that he would have counselled Mort, in that messing around with people's deaths is a sure way to get other people killed. There is a pattern to such deaths, and who knows what good may come of it.

Death's rural cultivating and harvesting lifestyle is threatened by a new device, a mechanical harvester, which threatens the livelihood of rural workers but not rural landowners. (There is of course a deeply symbolic threshing machine in Thomas Hardy's *Tess Of The D'Urbervilles* (1891).) Someday soon, even on the Discworld, such rural workers are going to be downsized.

Windle Poons is equally a fish out of water. Never having gone much further than his room and the dining room in his later years, now he is dead he can venture into new territory, even dangerous territory. The Shades holds no fears for one who is already dead. And curiously he is fitter than when he was alive. In fact, you'd say it was an act of homage to Harold Ramis' *Groundhog Day* (1993), if that film didn't get made later. His social circle widens to include bogeymen, vampires, werewolves and a wereman, each of whom offers a little minor key pastiche.

The Verdict: Not as well constructed as *Mort*, but the character of Death is just as moving, if not more so. Windle Poons' haunting is a bit of a retread of the hauntings from *Mort* (Princess Keli) and *Wyrd Sisters* (Verence). 3/5

Witches Abroad

Published: London: Gollancz, 1991.

Location: Lancre and the route to Genua, then Genua itself.

Story: The witch and fairy godmother Desiderata is about to die and needs an heir, in particular an heir to go on a mission to Genua to stop a girl from going to the ball and getting married. Curiously enough she latches onto Magrat as the best bet, although Granny Weatherwax and Nanny Ogg both see themselves as better holders of the wand. And particularly because Desiderata insisted that Magrat go alone, Granny and Nanny decide to go with her to Genua, which is what Desiderata would have wanted. Along the way they get the sense that someone is watching their every mood and trying to thwart their every move.

Major Targets: Our notions of the types of women and witches – the maiden, the mother and the crone. Fairy stories, especially *Cinderella*, *Rumpelstiltskin*, *Sleeping Beauty*, *Little Red Riding Hood*, *The Three Little Pigs* and *Goldilocks And The Three Bears* as well as a large dose of *The Wizard Of Oz*. These narratives are rural myths, the country cousins of urban myths, although rather than happening to a friend of a friend, they seem to happen all the time. Oh, and there's a cameo from Gollum, late of *The Hobbit*.

Cameos: Death: First to collect Desiderata, and then turning up at the ball. *The Librarian:* Doesn't seem to appear. *The Watch:* On the gates at Genua, and contrasted with the Ankh-Morpork equivalent. *Witches:* Well, obviously, yes, with further evidence that most of what they do is headology rather than magic. In addition to Desiderata, our thrilling threesome and various Lancre witches, there is Lily Weatherwax, Granny's long-lost sister, and the voodoo queen, Mrs Gogol. *Wizards:* Mentioned in comparison with witches and for their hats (although strangely not in relation to the Oz riff that runs through part of the novel). *Greebo:* His biggest appearance so far, as Nanny Ogg can't face leaving him behind (something that Jason Ogg is no doubt pleased about). He is a minor terror en route, but seems to meet his match in the voodoo cockerel Legba. Greebo is transformed into a human: hairy, eye-patched, leather-shirted, lecherous and a mean fighter into the bargain. *Vampires:* At one of the inns the witches stay in on the journey, Greebo notices a bat, which is after all only a mouse with wings and is clearly fair game. He doesn't realise that this is in fact a vampire bat and, whilst vampires can rise from the grave, they have severe difficulties in rising from a cat. *CMOT Dibbler:* In mail-order form only, as Magrat's supplier of useless goods and wisdom under the name of Grand Master Lobsang Dibbler.

Subtext: Another narrative where stories come to the fore; Genua itself is in the power of fairy stories, forcing the skivvy Emberella to marry against her will. This is not the only story, as the witches stumble upon *Sleeping Beauty* and *Little Red Riding Hood*, bringing their own particular logic to bear in dealing with such narratives. (Increasingly Discworld characters are prisoners of narrative imperatives and find themselves forced to behave in such a way as they would if they were in a story. See for example the point where the Watch increases the odds so that it is a million to one chance, and therefore might (must) just work. *The Science Of Discworld* includes the element of narrativium.) The narratives are presumably evidence of Lily Weatherwax's passage through those areas, or her current defences around the area she rules. As a defence against the arrival of the three witches, she throws a house at them part-way along a yellow brick road, which is a cue for some Munchkin-like dwarfs to come and demand ruby slippers.

Lily, or Lilith, is Esme Weatherwax's elder sister, the double name suggesting: an ambiguity between a flower symbolic of purity, in Jewish Talmudic tradition the first wife of Adam, synonymous with evil, or in the Old Testament, an Assyrian female demon of the night. Lilith was thrown out of the family many years before, forcing Esme to become a good witch, missing out on all the fun. It is quite difficult to take this seriously, since there is definitely a critique of bad witches running through the book and the series. Lilith and, worse than her, Black Aliss are held up as examples of what happens when witches try to have too much power, especially when using sorcery and enchantment on others. Nanny and Magrat watch in horror as Granny sits down to play cards to win back the money and broom that Nanny had lost: will she use magic to get her way, with all sorts of implications for how the witches will get treated from then on? Instead she uses the headology that ensures that people do what you want them to, of their own free will, whether they like it or not.

The power of magic brings with it a certain responsibility, and good or evil is as much a product of the user's intention as the spell itself. The character of Mrs Gogol is perhaps a little dubious, especially with all that consorting with the dead, but her heart is in the right place compared to Lily's.

The Verdict: Great fun. 5/5

Small Gods

Published: London: Gollancz, 1992.

Location: At the hub dwelling of the God and the history monks, and then in Omnia and Ephebe.

Story: Lu-Tze travels to Omnia to be witness to great events: the novice Brutha in the Church of Om is visited by the God Om in the form of a tortoise. Om is down to just one true believer, Brutha, and needs to gain more in order to survive even as a minor deity. Unfortunately Brutha comes to the attention of Vorbis, head of the Quisition, and embroiled in his plans to invade and convert Ephebe and neighbouring countries. Can Brutha survive the machinations of Vorbis and deal with the hourly blasphemies of his God?

Major Targets: Organised religion, in particular the Catholic Church and the Inquisition. Brutha, with his photographic memory, and the rôle of torture in the world echoes Gene Wolfe's *The Book Of The New Sun* (1980-83) sequence. The sea journey has echoes of Samuel Taylor Coleridge's *The Rhyme Of The Ancient Mariner* and the *Book Of Jonah* from the *Old Testament*. In Ephebe many of the details of the philosophy echo Greek philosophy – in particular Archimedes, Xeno and Diogenes, who as Didactylos bears an uncanny resemblance to taxi drivers. And there are echoes of the Cave of Plato's philosophy.

Cameos: Death: He collects a number of souls. We also revisit the Death of Rats, from *Reaper Man*. *The Librarian:* A brief appearance, to collect books from the fire at the Library of Ephebe. Quite how he gets there isn't certain. *CMOT Dibbler:* Or, rather, a close cousin, Cut-Me-Own-Hand-Off Dibblah.

Subtext: A number of the early *Discworld* novels feature young protagonists coming of age, and then being left behind at the end of the novel. Certainly the innocent and the innocent abroad – which could be extended to include Rincewind and Twoflower – hold a privileged place in Pratchett's oeuvre. In *Small Gods* the pattern is subtly different.

Brutha, the main character, ought to be the innocent abroad, who learns from his experiences and makes comic mistakes. But his strong sense of belief and photographic memory mean that whilst he does face perils in his journeys, he never seems to be in danger or in over his head. The character well out of his depth is his ostensible creator and master, Om, a God who has much to learn about himself and the way that he appears to others. Brutha can continue, safe in his faith, whether there is an Om to pray to or not. Om, on the other hand, needs believers. By the end of the novel he is a much-reformed deity, with much-improved commandments.

Through the course of the novel, Brutha rises from lowly novice to head of his church, but then being on speaking terms with God clearly helps. Whilst the events which lead to his meteoric rise are depicted over around four hundred pages, his stint as leader passes in a couple of hundred words. Presumably Pratchett's other protagonists grow old and die, but that usually happens off-stage. But here a death brings another appearance of death and discussion of the afterlife, and allows for the redemption of Vorbis, last seen (dead) crawling through the desert toward paradise.

The Quisition is a source of some satire but, because this is a comedy of not too macabre a shade, we are only told about some of the tools of the trade rather than seeing them in action for more than a few moments. In a neat inversion of the real-world Inquisition's interrogation of people like Galileo, the Church of Om believes that the Earth is a perfect sphere rather than being flat, on the back of four elephants, stood on the top of a turtle swimming through space. The heretics, quite rightly and logically in this context, argue that if the world were a sphere, then all the oceans would sink to the southern hemisphere and fall off (although this conveniently ignores whatever mechanism allows water to flow off the edge of the disc and be reconstituted as rain, presumably somewhere in the hub – that's magic, I guess).

The Verdict: A rich and deep novel. 5/5

Lords And Ladies

Published: London: Gollancz, 1992.

Location: Lancre and its surroundings, and briefly the Unseen University at Ankh-Morpork.

Story: Magrat returns from Genua to discover that Verence is arranging their marriage, which has sort of been on the cards since *Wyrd Sisters*. Hwel has even written a play for the occasion, on Midsummer's Night, which even now the rude mechanicals of the Lancre Morris men are rehearsing. And across at Unseen University a nostalgic Archchancellor Ridcully, Ponder Stibbons, an increasingly crazed Bursar and a theatre-loving orang-utan librarian have decided to attend. Unfortunately at Midsummer's Eve the fabric between the universes is at its weakest; the elves are poised to break through and invade with the unwitting aid of young women who are trying to become witches by dancing around a stone circle.

Major Targets: Our image of elves and elfish behaviour. The narrative of *A Midsummer Night's Dream* and a speech from *Henry V*. Wedding preparations.

Cameos: Death: Having his horse shod by Jason Ogg and collecting a soul. *The Librarian:* Travels to the wedding and bags the front row of the theatricals, armed with a bag of peanuts. *The Watch:* In Lancre it's just Shaun. *Witches:* The three we've come to know, Ogg, Weatherwax and Garlick, and some wannabes including Perdita (Agnes Nitt) and Diamanda (Lucy Tockley). *Wizards:* Ponder and Ridcully. *Greebo:* He seems to do little more than sleep on Nanny Ogg's bed, although he is a deadly weapon when kept in a box which someone is told not to open. (See *Johnny And The Dead* for Schrödinger's Cat). *Unseen University:* An early setting, before the wedding guests set out.

Subtext: There's an author's note here, reminding the reader that there were three earlier witches novels, which the reader ought to have read first. By now, of course, the Discworld is beginning to fill up (and the first map, of the layout of Ankh-Morpork, was published) and so Pratchett has to really worry about continuity errors. He has the continual problem of deciding whether to invent new characters (which old readers have to get to know and which involves continual invention) or to continue on with old ones (which new readers have to get to know and who have to be consistent with earlier appearances). All the witches have pasts – Magrat with Verence, Nanny Ogg with her three official husbands and the recurring Romeo dwarf character Casununda, and Granny Weatherwax who might have the Granny as an honorary title or might have a family we haven't yet seen.

With the best will in the world, witching seems to be a single woman's game (Nanny is presumably a widow or divorcée, several times over) and Magrat's dalliance with Verence requires her to give up such activities. Unless she wants to become a Witch Queen, but she's far too nice for that. She does resist becoming queen for a long time, although it does give her different power from that she had as a witch, and perhaps she will finally use the headology that Nanny and Granny swear by. Nevertheless, by the end of the book she is married off and presumably no longer going to be available for maiden duties (assuming Verence has worked out what to do).

Granny, rather surprisingly, turns out to have a past, one which involves a wizard, a wizard who now seems to regret that he went off to wizard and didn't marry her fifty or so years earlier. Granny, knowing all about nostalgia and what-might-have-been, views it differently and figures that a union might have been disastrous, and they were better off apart.

Nevertheless, by the end of the novel the three witches are all paired off, which is the narrative logic of *Lords And Ladies'* quasi source, *A Midsummer Night's Dream*. Shakespearean comedy traditionally ends with marriages all round, with the disruption in the social fabric which has occurred during the play being healed, temporarily at least. Comedy ends at a marriage. This leaves Pratchett at a kind of narrative dead end, which is only resolvable by ensuring that he gets his witches and wizards single again as soon as possible, or where that fails, importing a new witch or wizard. By this point in the series, the personnel of Unseen University is very much settled down, but it is clear that there are no end of witches waiting in the wings.

The Verdict: One of the less satisfying witch novels but still good stuff. 4/5

Men At Arms

Published: London: Gollancz, 1993.

Location: Ankh-Morpork.

Story: Captain Vimes is preparing for his marriage to Lady Sybil Ramkin, and anticipates a retirement from twenty-five years on the City Watch. It is probably just as well that he is retiring, since Lord Vetinari has adopted a positive discrimination policy and has admitted Detritus (a troll, last seen in *Moving Pictures*) and Cuddy (a dwarf) to the guards. The speciesism of the city may just be combated, if the Watch can avoid pulling itself apart under the weight of accumulated prejudice. Fortunately there is a case to focus the senses: something has been stolen from the Assassin's Guild, and a number of bodies, including a dwarf and a clown, have been found in suspicious circumstances (which is to say, dead). Vimes is sure that there is a connection, if only he can stay single and sober enough to work it out.

Major Targets: Police procedural (including, possibly, *Columbo*), positive discrimination and, indeed, racism.

Cameos: Death: A couple of calls. *The Librarian:* Deeply suspicious of readers and a temporary member of the Watch. *The Watch:* Well, yes. It's also worth noting that two of the Watch get close enough for the Disc to tastefully move for them. *Wizards:* Only mentioned in passing, but the Archchancellor and the Bursar have speaking rôles. *Patrician Vetinari:* Knows more than he lets on – such as the present whereabouts of Leonard of Quirm – and part of the plot. Having set up a city that works – with everything from begging to clowning regulated by Guilds – he has the problem of controlling crime that cuts across such boundaries. And he's canny enough to manipulate Vimes to do his will. *Unseen University:* The chosen site of Vimes' nuptials. *Vampires:* One is the Ramkin family solicitor (and has been for centuries) and they also crop up as a suggestion for the next minority to recruit. *CMOT Dibbler:* Seen adapting to the increased rich cuisine that comes with immigrants; rat on a stick anyone? *Gaspode:* Busy trying not to be recognised as a talking dog.

Subtext: The above plot summary is misleading in that it downplays the rôle of Carrot as detective, as charismatic leader and as apparent heir. Go back to *Guards! Guards!*, where Carrot has joined the Watch having left his adoptive family of dwarfs behind. He had been found in suspicious circumstances, with a sword and other elements of kingship, but nothing was ever made of this, beyond it justifying why people were willing to listen to Carrot. He maintains this quality. The possibility that he may be the king is the criminal MacGuffin that drives the plot - a secret plan to restore a monarchy to Ankh-Morpork. (Compare this to *Guards! Guards!*, which has a similar premise, if a different candidate – which of course plays off Carrot's identity).

As is only right in Pratchett's oeuvre, Carrot rejects such explicit trappings of power and such a visible power position. At the same time it has to be noted quite how powerful he is, being able to quell potential riots when species enemies trolls and dwarfs meet on the street. His knowledge of city ordinance allows him to charm his way through the stickiest of situations. At the same time he is happy (or at any rate willing) to take a bullet for Vetinari.

And Vetinari's manoeuvrings are again on display, but pretty well endorsed by the logic of the narrative. Vimes is instructed by Vetinari not to investigate the theft from the Assassins' Guild and to leave the murders alone, and Vetinari knows full well that this is the thing to galvanise Vimes into action. It may look like the hard-working cop being bawled out by City Hall, and that Vimes has twenty-four hours to solve the case before being booted down to traffic duty (or rather retiring to get married) but Vetinari plays a cunning game. Greek etymology is played with to note the origin of the word 'police' in 'polis', the word for city (as in metropolis), and there's a sense of the Greek city with civic responsibility, participation in cults, rituals and festivals, and the upholding of law as being central to Carrot and Vimes' conceptions of their rôles. The police are men of the city. But, as Vetinari knows full well, 'politician' comes from a similar root (via the Latin, to be pedantic), and is thus equally rooted in the city.

It's worth noting that this book was published in the same year as *Johnny And The Dead*, part of the children's Johnny Maxwell trilogy that concerns itself with the politics of race relations among other political points. Whereas Yo-less' blackness is a difference from the dominant race in the novels, here racial difference is replaced by species difference; the few characteristics of the skin colour and shapes of the face which differentiate different races are as nothing to the differences between the trolls and the dwarfs. But such differences can, and should, be overcome. Just as he was to do in *Johnny And The Bomb*, Pratchett puts 'racist' comments in the mouths of otherwise decent characters, not to endorse their racism, but to force us to examine our own prejudices. Of course, by the end of the decade the Metropolitan Police, a distant and mundane cousin of the Watch, would be declared institutionally racist, although institutions do consist of individuals.

Of course, echoing *Guards! Guards!* Pratchett kills off a guard, and this time we care a bit more, but he isn't the most vivid of the characters in the novel. Oh, and Gaspode the wonder dog is back.

The Verdict: A politically savvy book. 4/5

Soul Music

Published: London: Gollancz, 1994.

Location: Llamedos (try reading it backwards, and cf. Llareggub in Dylan Thomas, *Under Milk Wood*), Death's Domain, Quirm and Ankh-Morpork.

Story: As his adopted daughter Ysabell and his former apprentice Mort die in an accident, Death becomes depressed and goes off to join the Klatchian Foreign Legion to forget. Susan Sto Helit, currently living at the Quirm College for Young Ladies, finds herself having to substitute for Death. In her rounds she comes across Imp Y Celyn, who has come to Ankh-Morpork from Llamedos to seek his fortune. This he is finding, in the form of music, and a new style of music with rocks in it. Wielding a magical, even possessed, guitar, he forms a band with a dwarf and a troll and rapidly becomes a star... Except that the Guild of Musicians is not best pleased with unauthorised music and he's probably forfeited his soul...

Major Targets: Narratives about girls' boarding schools, rock music post-Buddy Holly (Imp Y Celyn is translated into Little Bud of the Holly), especially The Beatles, The Who, The Sex Pistols and U2, Edgar Allan Poe (the Raven who refuses to say 'Nevermore,' and who was named Quoth by his wizard 'owner'), and Valkyries.

Cameos: Death: Spends most of the book AWOL, as is usual in his cycle of novels, grieving over his daughter. *The Librarian:* Briefly a keyboard player for the Band With Rocks In It. *The Watch:* A couple of walk-on scenes to remind us of the city works. *Wizards:* The Raven was attached to a wizard, and Ponder Stibbons appears along with other members of the faculty. *Patrician Vetinari:* He keeps an eye on things but doesn't get involved. *Unseen University:* Somewhat disrupted by the music. And somewhat disruptive itself, as the mysterious shop that appears with the magic guitar is also affected by its position near the University. *CMOT Dibbler:* Sets himself up as manager of the band.

Subtext: In *Moving Pictures* a new media gripped a section of the Discworld's population, and CMOT Dibbler erroneously thought that his particular talents could make money out of the process. And the Librarian abandons his books to get involved. Much the same thing happens here, although the music is arguably much more sinister and demonic than anything Holy Wood had to offer.

Unfortunately *Moving Pictures* had much more scope in terms of scenes and sequences to parody successfully in writing than *Soul Music* can hope to emulate; anyone hoping to parody musical conventions has the spectres of *The Rutles* and *This Is Spinal Tap* to contend with. Drummers probably have to die, but it's been done before. Buddy or Imp (a name which inspires a throwaway reference to 'American Pie' and the day the music died) is referred to as being elfish, which is presumably straining after Elvis, and one of the band's early gigs is at a Cavern Club (echoing the name of the Beatles' legendary venue) complete with a Liverpudlian accented manager. Many of the other jokes depend on rewriting song titles or band names (examples: The Whom, &U). Buddy's guitar may be possessed, but by rights he should have come across it at a crossroad attended by the Devil.

Alongside this, and barely integrated to it until the climax, are the twin narratives of Susan and her Grandfather, Death. Like Mort before her, she allows her personal feelings to interfere with doing her job, although such a charge seems unfair given that Death has disappeared to mourn. Her humanity serves to demonstrate Death's coldness and lack of taste (except for the colour black) and by now perhaps we've had all the teenagers coming of age that we can handle. Of course Susan doesn't come across so much as Death in drag as a half-hearted Goth. Maybe we needed to see more of the Valkyries.

But not all is lost though. Death remains one of Pratchett's most appealing creations, even though in the books centred on him he's much more likely not to be doing his job than doing it. The Klatchian Foreign Legion is amusing (if overplayed), as is Death drowning his sorrows and life among the down-and-outs. But the brave thing is that Pratchett has chosen to kill off the protagonists of a previous book, Mort and Ysabell, and manufactures a logic as to why they should stay dead when Death has time-travelling abilities.

The Verdict: Rather straining too much for the pun or allusion. 2/5

Interesting Times

Published: London: Gollancz, 1994.

Location: The home of the Gods, Ankh-Morpork, the Counterweight Continent and XXXX.

Story: The wizards receive a demand for the Great Wizzard (sic) to be sent to the Counterweight Continent, and at first they are stumped as to who he is. Fortunately (for them), the Librarian remembers the hat he has been keeping since the end of *Sourcery*, which once belonged to Rincewind. With the aid of their magical computer, Hex, they locate Rincewind, and then transport him to the Counterweight Continent where he is reunited, in turn, with Cohen the Barbarian and Twoflower. The Red Army, inspired by Twoflower's account *What I Did On My Holidays*, want to overthrow the ruling powers and are convinced that Rincewind is the only person to help them. Rincewind has another idea, largely involving running away. Meanwhile Cohen and a horde of other aged heroes have their own plans to defeat the ruler of the Forbidden Kingdom.

Major Targets: Our knowledge of Chinese culture from the last few thousand years.

Cameos: Death: Arrives in time for the battle, with the other three horsemen in tow. *The Librarian:* Brings Rincewind's hat to the attention of the other wizards – and it is clarified that he too is a wizard. *Wizards:* Safely in the Unseen University. *Cohen:* And half a dozen other toothless, barely continent heroes with a combined age of getting on for a thousand. *Unseen University:* A setting for the wizards, but we get to see what Ponder Stibbons has been up to, in the creation of an ant- and rat-driven clockwork computer, Hex. *Vampires:* Used by Rincewind to scare the enemy. *CMOT Dibbler:* In his own right (Rincewind eats three of his sausages, so glad is he to be back in Ankh-Morpork, and Twoflower misses his pies) and a quasi cousin, Disembowel-Myself-Honourably Dibhala.

Subtext: It has to be said, this book seems to be somewhat wrongheaded. *Pyramids* had barely been a *Discworld* novel at all, dependent as it was on satirising, parodying or pastiching what we know, or what we think we know, about Egypt, particularly ancient Egypt. *Interesting Times* does the same, for China, and a China before the Communist revolution in the twentieth century, with the Red Army being the revolutionary forces and *What I Did On My Holidays* standing in for Mao Tse-Tung's *Little Red Book*. The title is quasi Chinese in origin, as the epigraph to the book reminds us of the supposed Chinese curse 'May you live in interesting times.' Rincewind is back, for the first time since *Eric*, and in terms of continuity, the first time since *Sourcery*. (No one refers to the events of *Eric* here.) And alongside him is Twoflower.

But thereby lies the rub. Twoflower, with his glasses, his endless smile and politeness, and his need to take photographs of everything (albeit with a Discworld equivalent of the brownie box camera, with a real brownie painting the pictures) was surely established as the very model of a stereotypical Japanese tourist. The wall around the kingdom, the terracotta warriors and the Forbidden Kingdom are all Chinese traits, and so the image of Twoflower and his background clash.

Rincewind's character is such that he can hardly do anything except run away, and this means that all he can do is plead for his life, try to escape or, er, run away. After three or four books of this, well, his coming out on top despite himself is less than convincing.

This mustn't damn the book altogether, since the narrative thread of the various elderly heroes, being educated and guided by Ronald Saveloy, a former teacher who is trying to bring civilisation to them, is very well handled. Pratchett is able to have fun here (as he does with a couple of members of the City Watch) with the literalness of some people and the unfortunate consequences of figurative language. At the same time it can only be inferred that Cohen has had some dentistry or the dentures acquired in *The Light Fantastic* are working since he's lost the lisp.

There is also a political commentary, as the democratic system of the city state of Ankh-Morpork (one man one vote) comes into conflict with the totalitarian state of the Counterweight Continent. The seeds of self-destruction in such dictated states are demonstrated. The Counterweight Continent is evil only to the extent that it undermines the autonomy of the individual, and even the revolution doesn't quite shift this, as Rincewind becomes the puppeteer to the terracotta soldiers.

The Verdict: The magnificent (if aged) seven are fun. 2/5

Maskerade

Published: London: Gollancz, 1995.

Location: Briefly in Lancre, afterwards in Ankh-Morpork.

Story: Agnes Nitt, aka Perdita X Nitt (but secretly Perdita X Dream), has run away to the opera at Ankh-Morpork. Meanwhile Nanny Ogg is worried that Granny Weatherwax is not at her best without a third witch to boss around and abuse, and ponders whether Agnes might make a decent maiden for the threesome. She gets her wish to see Granny busy again when a royalty cheque for a cookbook accidentally goes to Granny rather than Nanny, the true author. Granny is incensed about the profits that the publishers have made and determines to go to Ankh-Morpork with Nanny to seek redress, and at the same time, since they're there, no skin off her nose, they'll check on how Agnes is getting on. Agnes, as it happens, it at the centre of a murder plot, with a homicidal ghost stalking the opera house.

Major Targets: Opera, stage musicals, especially *The Phantom Of The Opera*, *Evita* and *Cats*, and stage superstitions. The stagecoach ride to Ankh-Morpork perhaps owes a smidgen to John Ford's *Stagecoach*. I think there's also a touch of Hitchcock in the portrayal of the mild-mannered janitor Walter Plinge and the theatrical denouements.

Cameos: Death: First seen trying to persuade a swan to sing so it will die, and then to collect the souls of the recently murdered. *The Librarian:* Playing the organ, for peanuts (you pay peanuts, you get, er, apes). *The Watch:* Undercover at the opera we have Nobby, Detritus and one or two more. Commander Vimes is mentioned but not seen. *Witches:* Ogg and Weatherwax, without Magrat. *Wizards:* Mentioned in passing as disapproving of moveable type – after all you should use the same type to set spells as a work of romantic fiction. It'd be disrespectful, and anyway the type might remember. *Greebo:* Turns into a human again when in a tight corner (his molecules having remembered their previous transformation) and latter magicked into human shape to accompany Granny Weatherwax to the opera. He's been before, in cat shape, and proves partial to other people's chocolates. *Vampires:* As members of a law firm. *CMOT Dibbler:* Strangely absent; perhaps the clientele is above him.

Subtext: At the end of *Lords And Ladies* the three witches seemed to paired off. Magrat is off, doing her queening, and should by rights be pregnant with an heir for Verence. Gytha Ogg had been stepping out with Casununda and Esme Weatherwax had been reunited with Ridcully. Now Casununda is nowhere to be seen and Ridcully has appeared in a couple of books without mentioning his past. Nor does Granny find time to seek him out in the Unseen University, which is only a stone's throw from the opera house (well, rather more of a lob, really). As I suggested, such partners have to be dispensed with for the comedy to continue (note how Commander Vimes, also recently married, is absent from a speaking rôle).

Agnes Nitt is there again, as a young woman interested in magic but without the moral dubiousness of her one-time partner in magic, Diamanda, although now she seems to have troubles with her alter ego Perdita X taking over her personality. It's not quite *Strange Case Of Dr Jekyll And Mr Hyde*, since the ghost provides enough doubles without Perdita going on the rampage, but it's a potential seed for another story unless her power for magic is tapped.

Meanwhile we have the complex plots of operas – resembling real-world operas, and leaving us to infer that there are Discworld equivalents of Wagner (more Valkyries), Mozart and so forth – certainly the musical director Salzella offers an equivalent to Salieri. Of course the novel itself has a plot worthy of an opera, whilst also being a whodunnit; it is interesting to note quite how often reasonably recent *Discworld* novels are police procedurals on some level. Set against this are the possibility of stage musicals, from Rodgers & Hammerstein to Andrew Lloyd Webber, with *The Phantom Of The Opera* (which obviously predates Webber by a century) as a clear intertext.

With a dash of Alfred Hitchcock's *Psycho* (1960), Walter Plinge is set up as a mild-mannered janitor who knows more than he should and shows up more often than he should. Indeed, he seems the most likely candidate to be involved in something suspicious. The unmasking is perhaps closer to *Scooby Doo*, but without any mention of pesky kids.

It's worth remembering the scenes at the printer, to see how they foreshadow any details of *The Truth*; Mr Goodberger's name is an Anglicisation of Johannes Gutenberg (1398-1468), the inventor of movable type. Here the method would appear to be engraving, but it isn't entirely clear – and there's a neat joke about proofreading.

The Verdict: Back to form after a bit of a rut. 4/5

Feet Of Clay

Published: London: Gollancz, 1996.

Location: Ankh-Morpork.

Story: The ranks of the Watch continue to swell, with the addition of Cheery Littlebottom, a dwarf with a secret. And Commander Sir Samuel Vimes continues his enforced social climbing by having to visit the Royal College of Heraldry on Mollymog Street to pick up a Vimes coat of arms. Whilst he is there he discovers two things – that his ancestor Stoneface Vimes' execution of the last king of Ankh-Morpork means that the Vimes coat of arms has been permanently withdrawn and that Nobby is the descendant of Edward St John de Nobbes, Earl of Ankh-Morpork. But he barely has time to pay attention to such matters, because someone has poisoned Lord Vetinari. Meanwhile, there have been a number of other murders in the city, apparently involving golems, and this wouldn't be a realistic crime narrative if there wasn't some link between all this.

Major Targets: Police procedural, again, but it's pretty well simply a narrative by now. Cheery Littlebottom looks like being the Cracker of the

Discworld. Heraldry is parodied. At some point the possibility of Vetinari having been poisoned by a book, like in *The Name Of The Rose*, is raised.

Cameos: Death: Collects a murder victim. *The Librarian:* I might have missed him in person, but there's a mention of the Library and Vimes reading a book there. *The Watch:* The further adventures of the Watch. *Wizards:* Mentioned in relation to the high energy research building. *Patrician Vetinari:* In bed, suffering from the poison, and trying to work out how to let Vimes know what the cause is without hurting his feelings. Aaaah. *Unseen University:* As a location. *Vampires:* The dragon at the Royal College of Heraldry is a vampire, and Vimes draws the line at admitting them to the Watch.

Subtext: Funny—all the narratives based around the City Watch seem to involve an attempt to revive the lost kingship of Ankh-Morpork, and Vimes is possibly the most democratic of the officials in the city (he hates everyone equally). Vimes, as descendent of someone who executed the last king – a tyrant by all accounts, but even so, he *was* the king – has clearly inherited republicanism in his genes, and this makes his own ennoblement somewhat awkward for him. He's now superior in class to most people in the city, but viewed as jumped up by the nobility. He can't win.

This time it's not Carrot who is the choice for pretender, but Nobby, although the claim is ambiguous at best. It's clear that if he were to be restored to his Earldom, and thence to the kingship, he would just be a puppet in the hands of those who want power for themselves. Again there is a palpable sense that anyone who wants power for themselves is dangerous, but there is also the sense that people want others to have dominion over them.

Meanwhile there is the sub-plot of the golem. The clay made living automata is derived from Jewish mystical history. The golem are powered by words written on their foreheads, or here written on a piece of parchment and stuck inside their foreheads. With their total, unceasing, unthinking loyalty to a programmed master, the golem are a slave race, and one of the sub-plots involves their attempts at liberation. Some of the attempts at liberation are catastrophic, or suicidal.

And back in the palace there is Vetinari, who has lasted in power for as long as he has because he is the least worst option: none of the Guilds would trust another Guild to put forward a candidate to rule Ankh-Morpork. Poison is a traditional method of getting rid of unwanted rulers, although here it is a lot less successful than in real life. Vetinari's intelligence means that he works out the source of the poison long before Vimes does, but doesn't want to tell him because he doesn't want to undermine Vimes who is very useful indeed to him. In his investigation Vimes has annoyed several

Guilds, a number of races and a couple of organised religions, which is all to the good as far as Vetinari can see. Keep them divided and you keep them conquered. And, besides, Vimes can unwittingly do the dirty work Vetinari can't do himself.

The Verdict: Not one of the stronger Watch novels – personally I think there are so many watchmen (and women, and dwarfs, and...) that the characters are getting a bit diluted. 3/5

Hogfather

Published: London: Gollancz, 1997.

Location: Ankh-Morpork, Death's Domain, the Tooth Fairy's Palace of Bones and various other dimensional anomalies.

Story: The Auditors engage the Guild Of Assassins to kill the Hogfather, which will have the unfortunate consequence of ending reality as we know it. Teatime is the man for the job, and he will stop at nothing in his pursuit of anthropic personifications – including the Tooth Fairy, who clearly has a stash of money somewhere. (There's a line in *Lords And Ladies* about there being three such Fairies. Perhaps it's a franchise deal, perhaps the other two have retired.) With Hogswatchnight, er, dawning (dusking?) Death takes over the rôle of Hogfather and distributes presents across the world. Susan, currently a governess, is dragged into the metaphysical battle.

Major Targets: Christmas, but also other paranoiac belief systems – stolen socks, pencils, clean towels and so forth. A sly dig at *The X-Files*. Oh, and *Mary Poppins* and *A Christmas Carol*.

Cameos: Death: With a false beard and a cushion up his cloak and a rather false sounding HO HO HO. *The Librarian:* Goes to bed early on Hogswatchnight, and later emerges to play on the organ. *The Watch:* Corporals Nobby and Visit queue up for the Hogfather in a shop. *Wizards:* The usual cast, plus Sideney who has lost a wager and finds himself working for Teatime. *Unseen University:* As a setting – with a bathroom which has been brought back into use, the organ, a hall decked with mistletoe (but a lack of women, aside from Susan who is presumably off limits) and HEX again.

Subtext: Hogswatch is mentioned as far back as *The Colour Of Magic* in the *Discworld* series, and before that in *The Dark Side Of The Sun*, but this is the first time we see it celebrated properly. Obviously, it is a Discworld version of Christmas, but it harks back to the celebration of the winter solstice (and fears about the sun not coming back) as well as the Scottish Hogmany (New Year), and the various late night religious services or Watch Nights. The Christmas rituals themselves owe something to stories of St

Nicholas (not necessarily as nice a figure as we think) and to Odin, the Norse God.

The book becomes organised between the twin poles of belief and charity. Firstly the absence of the Hogfather leads to a surplus of belief, and it has long been established that belief has a powerful impact upon existence on the Discworld (think back to some of the dragons). The belief is rechannelled into figures that look after other aspects of life. We all know that socks go missing; well, now there is a God responsible. Mythology offers us Bacchus or Dionysus as the God of Wine – so it follows that there is Bilious, the Oh God of Hangovers, and so forth. It becomes clear that these fairy stories, or white lies, these everyday minor beliefs are necessary as limbering-up exercises to the big beliefs in big lies, such as justice and morality.

Meanwhile Hogswatchnight is seen as a time of giving and of charity, and of alleviating suffering for one night of the year. To which those who suffer the other days of the year can only cheer, half-heartedly. There's the old line about giving a man a fish and you feed him for one meal (although he probably has to pass it on to his wife to gut it and cook it), but give him a net and you feed him for life (EU fishing quotas notwithstanding). Acts of charity may only alleviate problems very briefly; for longer-term solutions a complete reconfiguration of the socio-economic system is required, as a number of the characters here acknowledge. So, do we not give to charity in the hope that the situation deteriorates so much that society collapses and major solutions are found? Or do we just stick a plaster over the problem? Ho, ho, ho, indeed.

Lighten Up Already: Ridcully is revealed as having a penchant for Wow-Wow Sauce, a marvellous condiment for bubble and squeak and an alleged hangover cure. In fact there is such a sauce, and here is one of the many recipes for it:

> 25g (1 oz) Butter.
> 25g (1 oz) Plain Flour.
> 300 ml (½ Pint) Beef Stock.
> 1 tbsp White Wine Vinegar.
> 1 tbsp Worcestershire Sauce.
> 1 tbsp Mustard.
> Salt and Pepper.
> 2-3 tbsp Chopped Parsley.
> 2 Diced Pickled Cucumbers.

First make a roux in a pan by melting butter and adding flour whilst stirring. Gradually add the stock to make a smooth sauce. Season with vinegar,

Worcestershire sauce and mustard and cook gently for 20 minutes with the lid on. Season to taste. Carefully stir in the parsley and pickled cucumbers. Heat through and serve. (Some recipes also call for a mushroom purée.)

Maybe I've had too many hot curries, but I made it and it wasn't that spicy. But you can get some marvellous chilli oils these days...

The Verdict: Remarkably cosmic, but stops being comic. Inventive rather than side-splitting. 3/5

Jingo

Published: London: Gollancz, 1997; the last Gollancz hardback before Pratchett moved to Doubleday.

Location: On the site of Leshp, Ankh-Morpork, Klatch and areas between.

Story: Two fishermen are startled by the reappearance of the lost island of Leshp (last mentioned in *Mort*) from three hundred fathoms beneath the sea, but not startled enough to fail to claim the land for Ankh-Morpork. Unfortunately two Klatchians are in the area and have the same idea. Meanwhile Commander Vimes is leading the procession at a state visit of Prince Khufurah and spots a would-be assassin taking aim at the visitors. It is clear that the assassination attempt has been engineered to cause more mistrust between Ankh-Morpork and Klatch, but also that it has been engineered to be clear. Lord Rust usurps Lord Vetinari and declares a state of war. As Vimes and Carrot chase 71-Hour Ahmed, the Prince's bodyguard, and Angua across the sea to Klatch, Nobby and Colon find themselves with Leonard of Quirm and Lord Vetinari in a submarine. It is clear that bloodshed will ensue unless someone can restore law and order pretty damn pronto.

Major Targets: War – in all its forms, from medieval battles to the Gulf War, via the First World War and the Falklands. But worse than that, patriotism and the attitudes which led to women handing out white feathers to those men who did not go to war in 1914-1918. Unthinking racism. The arms-for-Iraq scandal has a cameo, as does the magic bullet theory, a book depository and the assassination of John F Kennedy, even down to the grassy knoll (or rather a gnoll that grasses). The subtly different shades of religious belief. For light relief *Das Boot* and *Lawrence Of Arabia*.

Cameos: Death: Remarkably few appearances, given the number of deaths (all but two off-stage). And not a horseman in sight. *The Librarian:* Very briefly, recalling his rôle as a special constable in the Watch. *The Watch:* The novel centres on them, although they are somewhat split up. *Wizards:* They turn up to the trial of Lord Vetinari. *Patrician Vetinari:* A larger rôle than usual, trying to keep peace, make war, no doubt make a profit, and to keep Vimes behaving in exactly the way Vetinari wants him to. *Unseen University:* Setting for the state visit, and for investigations of the assassination attempt. *CMOT Dibbler:* Briefly, and Klatch Al Djibla is clearly a distant cousin.

Subtext: Many of the earlier *Discworld* novels were *Bildungsromans*: a young character being tossed into a difficult situation and finding the strength within themselves to survive and triumph. Children are banished from *Jingo*, as the potentially serious subject of war re-enters Pratchett's palette (after a narrowly avoided skirmish in *Pyramids*). Given the context of the 1990s and the *Discworld*, this offers us everything we thought we knew about the Gulf War, with the assassination of JFK and the David Lean biopic *Lawrence Of Arabia* thrown in for good measure. Captain Vimes views both assassination and war as crimes, and so it is part of his brief to solve and stop them. By now the City Watch regulars seem to have replaced the Witches in Pratchett's repertoire and certainly their antics are enjoyable enough to read about.

The *Lawrence Of Arabia* parallels best display the strengths and weaknesses of this novel. Pratchett's strength lies in an elasticity of realism. At one point Vimes holds a burning ember in his hand: 'The trick is not to mind that it hurts.' Peter O'Toole played the same trick in 1962, but here it's undercut by Vimes obviously minding: 'Damn damn damn! Has anyone got any cold water?' The novel contains dozens of moments such as this; but at the same time, a four-decade-old movie hardly seems a brave target for satire. Similarly, despite Saddam Hussein's best efforts since the US invasion, the Gulf War and the supergun affair have made that transition from current affairs to recent history that means the satirical parody is a toothless pastiche—nostalgically amusing in its own way, but too comfortable to change or challenge the world. There are moments when, thanks to the Trousers Of Time, we can glimpse a different path, when the Watch die in 'glorious' battle. But this is not *Blackadder Goes Forth*—the comedy pulls back from confronting the reality of war, so we have a football match transplanted from c. 1914 (when the war was obviously *not* going to be over by Christmas) to replace a battle.

Of course Pratchett's essential humanism means that he's more interested in war by other means than in war itself. The speciesism of Ankh-Morpork has long been rife, but here the anti-Klatchian feelings mirror an earlier age's anti-German or anti-Japanese bias. Vimes, in a move which anticipates supposed police anxieties after the report into the Stephen Lawrence case, sees a Klatchian as shifty, but is not allowed to see him as shifty because he's a Klatchian, i.e. there should be no causal link between his nationality and his status. At the same time Vimes' own prejudices in his dealings with 71-Hour Ahmed are presented as honesty rather than racism.

The book's title comes from GW Hunt's music hall song 'By Jingo', which dates from the 1870s, a period of anti-Russian feeling:

> We don't want to fight,
> But by Jingo if we do,
> We've got the ships,
> We've got the men,
> And got the money too.
> We've fought the Bear before,
> And while we're Britons true,
> The Russians shall not have Constantinople.

In other words, access to the Mediterranean. The words of the song are (mis)quoted in the novel itself.

But with all these criticisms in mind, let it be said that it's a book to return to and ponder its implications. The Klatchians are set up as a Discworld version of the Arabs, whose leaders wish to unite them in the face of a common enemy. At the same time, references to Vindaloo and shopkeeping position them as Indians or Pakistanis. Is this meshing together of nationalities, this any-foreigner-will-do for satire attitude, xenophobic? Or is it a representation of Klatch itself as a flag of convenience for a number of nationalities? *The Discworld Companion* suggests that Klatch as continent (rather than as a country) includes Tsort, Djelibeybi, Ephebe and Omnia. And Constable Visit is of Omnian stock. Divided loyalties.

It's worth paying attention to the images of wind, and the smells they bring with them, and the almost final image of a statue of Stoneface Vimes, somewhere out of the wind.

The Verdict: A novel which grows in stature on rereading. 3/5 on first reading, 5/5 subsequently

The Last Continent

Published: London: Doubleday, 1998.

Location: Unseen University, a desert island and XXXX, the last continent.

Story: The Librarian has caught a disease which means that he is continually changing shape. Disconcerted and worried by this, the wizards decide to try and change him back from an orang-utan (or red furry deckchair, as may be) to a humanoid, but unfortunately for this they need his real name, and none of them can remember it. Indeed, all the records appear to have vanished. They are convinced that Rincewind would know it, but first they have to find him, which through a combination of bad luck and stupidity leaves them stranded on a desert island. Rincewind, meanwhile, finds himself trying to survive in a place not totally unlike Australia.

Major Targets: Australiana: *The Adventures Of Priscilla, Queen Of The Desert, Mad Max*, Vegemite, pie and peas, Peach Melba, beer, *Crocodile Dundee*, "no worries, mate," and *Desert Island Discs*.

Cameos: Death: Takes a rather puzzled look at Rincewind's hourglass of life. *The Librarian:* Somewhat under the weather. *Wizards:* Trapped on a desert island, trying to deal with the real world and having a woman around. *Unseen University:* Arguably the wizards never leave it, since they've climbed through the office window of one of the faculty to get to the desert island, but that way lies multidimensional madness, particularly as they are somewhere back in time and might murder their grandfathers (not that they have anything against elderly relatives, it's just something that happens when you meddle with causality). *CMOT Dibbler:* Rincewind meets the XXXX equivalent and recalls a couple of dozen national varieties.

Subtext: We've already had Discworld versions of Egypt and China, and here the action moves to Australia – as set up at the end of *Interesting Times*, which was the last book to feature wizards. What do we know about Australia, or think we know? Uluru (or Ayers Rock as it was known, briefly, for a couple of centuries), kangaroos, Dame Edna, emu, Sydney Opera House and *Neighbours* and *Home And Away*? Australia's a young country, independent for a century but still nominally under the British constitutional monarchy. It consists of a terrain ranging from the virtual isolation of the red centre to the cityscapes of Melbourne and Sydney, cities which have served as SF sets in an increasing number of movies. The road itself was the star in *Mad Max* and *Priscilla*. Equally, there is the aboriginal population. In a number of books Pratchett makes the point about the politics of countries being discovered; the people already living there not being aware that it was particularly lost.

Here we have Rincewind running though the red interior, dealing with kangaroo and beer, inventing Vegemite and Peach Melba, and finding himself the centre of a folk ballad that has echoes of Ned Kelly, an Australian bush ranger folk hero, who wore home-made armour. The humour here depends on how many Antipodian references we can spot, and how quickly Pratchett can move Rincewind through the landscape. In other words, situation normal for Rincewind.

Meanwhile there is the narrative of the wizards – including Ridcully, the Bursar and Ponder Stibbons, along with the Librarian – inadvertently trapped on a desert island. The island is a new creation (but then they are back in time) and is the province of a God who is still creating it. Virtually everything they desire is created and it seems like paradise. Still, they do need to leave. Life is made uncomfortable by the presence of the head housekeeper of Unseen University, Mrs Whitlow, who is already the centre of what passes for erotic fantasies among some of the faculty. The sight of a sunbathing, semi-naked woman is as shocking as a streaker might have been at Queen Victoria's Golden Jubilee.

The *Discworld* series began with wizards, in particular with Rincewind, and there is no doubt the books are very popular. Pratchett is presumably forced to return to a favourite creation. But the university is not set up for the sort of narratives that, say, David Lodge has been able to sustain, and Rincewind does nothing but run away. I've written that already, of course, but then he keeps on doing it.

The Verdict: Better on rereading, but the wizards and Rincewind are rather limited in scope, even away from the university. Actually, in some of the early pages here, there are some rather good jokes about universities and the habits of students, but that's probably a personal prejudice of mine. 2/5

Carpe Jugulum

Translation Of Title: 'Go for the throat,' on the model of Carpe Diem, 'Seize the day.'

Published: London: Doubleday, 1998.

Location: Lancre.

Story: Magrat has given birth to a daughter and wants Esme Weatherwax to be the godmother. But life never goes smoothly. For a start, Granny has vanished off somewhere, possibly in a huff, and even worse the kingdom has been invaded by vampires with modern ideas. These are Vampires who have slowly acclimatised to all the sorts of things one usually uses to kill a vampire – holy water, garlic, daylight... Can the newly-formed coven of Agnes/Perdita Nitt, Magrat Garlick and Nanny Ogg defeat the vampires, even with the help of Om proselytiser Mightily Oats? Or should Magrat just agree to be bitten and stab the vampires in the middle of the night?

Major Targets: Vampire narratives and folklore about witches.

Cameos: Death: Visits Granny Weatherwax and almost helps out as she deals with the dilemma of saving a mother or a child. It might be an ongoing effect of the Trousers Of Time, but this book and the next (when Death visits Vimes) seems to be edgier– people might die or not. *The Watch:* In Lancre, Shawn Ogg appears to be it. *Witches:* The dynamics of the coven seem to be explored in the most depth in this volume. *Wizards:* Nanny mentions knowing a wizard many years ago; this presumably should not be confused with Granny's affair with Ridcully or is a continuity error. *Greebo:* Still around in cat form and found asleep on the throne at one point. An angry cat would appear to be the best defence against a vampire. *Patrician Vetinari:* Mentioned in passing as referring to 'werewolf economies,' a cousin of tiger economies. *Vampires:* This is not the first appearance of vampires in the sequence (there is a recurring lawyer character who is a vampire) but this is the first time they've occupied narrative centre stage. They also have Igor, a conflation of the Frankenstein monster and the mad scientist's assistant from the Universal horror movies of the 1930s and their many parodies. Igor, or possibly his relative Igor (oh, and Igor, Igor and Igor), also appears in *The Fifth Elephant*.

Subtext: The witches' coven is based around the supposed three stages of womanhood: the maiden, the mother and the crone. When the coven was first established in *Wyrd Sisters* and then *Witches Abroad*, Magrat was the wet hen who made the tea, Nanny the matriarch and Granny the old biddy – although the latter was by far the strongest of the three, in terms of her own powers and as a character. With Magrat's attachment to Verence in *Lords And Ladies* and *Maskerade*, the maiden status was clearly under threat; Pratchett was able to have a number of jokes about marital aids and sex manuals, but sooner or later the married couple would have to do *it*, and Magrat would be a maiden no more. With the witches latching on to Agnes, it seemed as if a replacement maiden was available. But was Magrat out of the loop altogether? It could be that Magrat gets to be the mother, and Nanny promoted to crone, and Granny is made somewhat redundant.

Alternatively, this might simply be what Granny wants them to believe, as a long-term ploy for defeating vampires.

Granny spends much of the book helped by Mightily Oats, a member of the Church of Om, an official initially called in to perform the naming ceremony for Magrat's child. The witches have reason to fear the Church of Om, since in olden times they didn't suffer witches to live. Or, rather, they made sure witches suffered whilst they died at the stake. Granny's common sense headology is pitched against Oats' personal philosophy, and he emerges as a more reasonable person than a member of an oppressive organised religion might be expected to, given Pratchett's ongoing critique of power structures. It is the organisation, of course, that is dangerous, not necessarily the individual.

Agnes' schizophrenic status proves useful again to the narrative. Whilst everyone else seems to fall under the spell of one or more of the vampires, when Agnes is captured Perdita can take over the body, and vice versa.

Not since *Small Gods* or *Lords And Ladies* has Pratchett dealt which such palpable evil, an evil which blurs the edges of what is seen as moral. It is very persuasive (especially given the uneasy equation the sequence sets up between species and ethnic minorities) just to think of the vampires as individuals who are misunderstood, or the victims of prejudice. But their usurpation of the power of other individuals marks them out as evil; as a counterpart to this Granny Weatherwax is revealed to be the granddaughter of Black Aliss, a witch that went to the bad. Good and evil might sometimes be a matter of attitudes, but at the same time there are absolutes. If Granny is no longer the crone, and has rejected Black Allis, has her narrative come to an end? Pratchett comes close here to killing her off but steps back – but for how long?

The Verdict: Another confrontation with pure evil. 5/5

The Fifth Elephant

Published: London: Doubleday, 1999.

Location: Ankh-Morpork but mostly in Überwald.

Story: Vetinari sends Commander Vimes as the Duke of Ankh-Morpork, along with his wife, to Überwald to participate in the coronation of the new dwarf Low King and to act as an ambassador in trade talks. Carrot resigns from the Watch, to try and track down Angua, who has gone missing, so the only choice to take over the Watch in Vimes' absence is Sergeant Fred Colon. Within days the Watch have been decimated, and the remaining staff are on strike. Back in Überwald, Vimes becomes embroiled in dwarf politics, and attempts to investigate the theft of the Scone of Stone, a replica of which had been stolen from the dwarf museum in Ankh-Morpork.

Major Targets: Locked room mysteries, diplomacy, ambassadors and their receptions, telecommunications, royal pomp, working conditions, and a slice of Chekhov.

Cameos: Death: Visits Vimes as he finds himself on the run from werewolves (it's a long story). *The Watch:* Initially seen on traffic duty (with Nobby still in drag from *Jingo*), then investigating theft. Detritus and Littlebottom go to Überwald with Vimes, a troll and a feminine dwarf being Vetinari's idea of diplomacy. *Patrician Vetinari:* Sends Vimes on the mission and appoints Colon as head of the Watch. He has a reason for doing everything. *Vampires:* Überwald is home to vampires and werewolves, alongside the dwarfs. The vampires seen here are friendlier than the ones in *Carpe Jugulum*; the Ankh-Morpork vampires apparently work in kosher butchers.' *Gaspode:* Finds himself running with wolves.

Subtext: Pratchett continues to mine new territory, if only through coming so close to killing off a major character (just as he did in *Carpe Jugulum*). I've already suggested that comedy can be derived from the failure of actions or reality to match up to desires, and that marriage is often the end of a comic sequence – married couples can be the source of comedy, but it is rare for major characters to be followed through from bachelorhood to life after getting married – after all, old age and death can only follow. Vimes was single when we met him, but then married Lady Sybil. The comedy of the marriage derives from the class inequalities between Sybil's equals and Vimes', as well as her attempts to mould him into being more of a figure-head, not running off to solve a crime at any opportunity. Of course, marriage brings a further narrative problem, if realism is to be observed. Sooner or later an heir has to be produced, and so far Lady Sybil has seemed more interested in dragons than in the pitter-patter of tiny feet. Well, this seems set to change thanks to the narrative here.

Of course, the Watch sequence has often been about heirs, in particular heirs to the lost throne of Ankh-Morpork - usually Carrot or some other unwitting pretender. *The Fifth Elephant* is no exception, but here it is the dwarf throne rather than the Ankh-Morpork one which is in question. Carrot is more concerned with his own relationship with Angua and how this will impact on his life. As a human adopted by dwarfs his species identity is of course fluid, and the impact of a hard line dwarf Low King, with its rejection of the humanised dwarfs who have moved to Ankh-Morpork, will strike home personally.

In some ways, though, Carrot need not worry. Just as Vetinari is the master of diplomacy, manipulation and the secret scheme, so even the dwarfs who appear to take back to basics, stay out of daylight or sing about gold policies, realise that the species is still living within the context of the wider world. Some things are worth saying, whilst actions speak differently. Idealism and pragmatism are in constant battle, but it is pragmatism that seems to be winning here. (This attitude might be compared to Grimma's early encounter with Abbot in *Truckers*.)

This conflict might include the status of Scone of Stone, a Discworld equivalent of the Stone of Scone, once incorporated into the coronation chair of England but eventually returned to Scotland. The Stone was the Stone of Destiny, on which the ancient Scottish kings were crowned, and serves as a mark of continuity, and the legitimate passage of power from one generation to the next. If it is actually the real stone, then as long as this isn't general knowledge it doesn't really matter. Equally, the transference of power probably isn't legitimate but if enough people believe it, then everything is hunky-dory.

Vimes remains viable as a character because he has enough self-knowledge to see through the power games, enough honesty to cut through the obfuscation, and enough common sense not to impose the truth on the rest of the population. His skills as an ambassador consist of being brutally honest or of pushing racism to the nth degree (although he may not necessarily believe in it). We have seen this in his dealings with nobles in *Jingo*, and before that in *Men At Arms*. And being descended from a king killer helps, too.

The Verdict: A complex, at times frightening, novel. 4/5

The Truth

Published: London: Doubleday, 2000.

Location: Ankh-Morpork.

Story: William de Worde writes a newsletter for various nobles around the Discworld and decides to move into business with dwarfs, using movable type. Having moved into mass (well, a couple of hundred) production, he begins to rake in the money. The first daily Discworld newspaper is born – and the Guild of Engravers is not happy. Meanwhile more sinister plans are afoot – someone is plotting to replace Vetinari as Patrician, and Mr Pin and Mr Tulip have been called in to do the job. Before long Commander Vimes of the Watch has two problems on his hands: the chaos caused by newsprint resulting in Guild rivalries, and an attempted murder committed by Vetinari.

Major Targets: Newspapers and printing. Gangsters – there is a whiff of *Pulp Fiction* about Mr Pin and Mr Tulip. Deep Throat and the Watergate scandal. E-commerce.

Cameos: Death: Briefly, and taking a surprisingly active rôle in determining the afterlife. *The Watch:* Angua, Nobby, Carrot and Littlebottom have brief appearances, and Vimes comes into conflict with William, but they are all uncomfortably sidelined by the narrative. Igor is now working for the Watch. *Wizards:* Mentioned briefly, but not as prominent as you'd expect given the wizardly mistrust of the printed word. *Patrician Vetinari:* And a double, briefly. He is of course very much aware of the power of the printed word, but as long as CMOT Dibbler isn't involved he's not too bothered. There is a clever exchange on the notions of what interests the public and what is in the public's interest. Once the Patrician is embroiled in the plot, he rather slips away from the narrative. The network of communications which in the last few books had been used for sending claxes now offers a chance for economic exploitation, and Vetinari is very much aware of this. But so-called c-commerce doesn't quite emerge in this volume. *Vampires:* The newspaper employs Otto as a photographer, which is suicidal given that the bright flash of the salamander kills vampires. Fortunately vampires can usually be resuscitated. *CMOT Dibbler:* He sees the possibilities of newspapers and finds employment as the writer of the Discworld version of the *National Enquirer*. *Gaspode:* As informant.

Subtext: Back in *Maskerade* Nanny Ogg had been published by Goodberger's firm, although then it was not clear whether the method was movable type and typesetting, or whether it was a process of engraving and printing from plates. By now the dwarfs have developed printing presses where the individual letters of each word are typeset and corrections can be made mid-printrun. OK, so it's state of the art c. 1600, but it still feels as if the Discworld is entering into a modern period. (More advanced printing had been achieved before on the Counterweight Continent, but they're foreigners and don't count.) Communication between cities is now possible by mechanical rather than magical means, and we've already seen union activity (as opposed to Guild activities) in *The Fifth Elephant*.

William de Worde was mentioned in *The Discworld Companion* as the creator of form letters for dwarfs to write home to their families with, and it is noted that his services have been used by the Duke of Sto Helit, King Verence II (the former fool) and the Seriph of Al Khali among others. However, he hasn't previously appeared as a character in his own right; perhaps he's been waiting for the right narrative to come along.

Meanwhile Gaspode, who had a rôle in *The Fifth Elephant* and was last seen going down a river (on a boat), has made it back to Ankh-Morpork and is surviving as only he knows how, making money from the curious incident of Vetinari's dog in the night-time. His Deep Throat act, and his disguise to prevent his capture because both the Watch and the evil Mr Pin and Mr Tulip are seeking a terrier, are two of the highlights of the books. It's also worth noting how his exchange of money for information echoes William's own career and ushers in the period of the information age.

At the risk of giving the plot away, it is rather a shame that we are unlikely to see more of Mr Pin and Mr Tulip. There is a sense that they've walked out of a Tarantino script, complete with violence, swearing and the Discworld equivalent of a debate about what the French call a Quarter Pounder with Cheese.

Note how this is another narrative about the conspiracies surrounding succession, except that this time it is the Patrician who is being succeeded, not a king. But note also how sidelined the Watch is from the narrative and its resolution. I suspect the point is to make us think twice about Vimes' character – is he really a bastion of freedom or as corrupt as Vetinari?

The Verdict: Sidelining the Watch like this and then having a mystery narrative is rather disappointing. 3/5

Thief Of Time

Published: London: Doubleday, 2001

Location: Death's Domain, a monastery and Ankh-Morpork.

Story: Death is alarmed to discover that time is going to end next Wednesday and seeks the help of Susan to discover what's going on, as well as trying to round up the other Horsemen of the Apocalypse for one last ride. Meanwhile in the monastery of the History Monks, Lu-Tze or the Sweeper takes on a new novice, Lobsang Ludd, with remarkable time-slicing skills. And in Ankh-Morpork clockmaker Jeremy Clockson is approached to make the most accurate clock ever. Could these things be connected? Do, as Susan wonders, bears poo in the woods?

Major Targets: Some material on time paradoxes and subdividing time. Various martial arts movies, including *The Matrix*. A group of characters are assigned aliases (and bicker about them) rather like in *Reservoir Dogs*.

Cameos: Death: Discovering history is going to end, and then rounding up the old team. *The Librarian and The Watch:* Nowhere to be seen. *Witches:* Nanny Ogg has a few appearances over the years. *Wizards:* A project is mentioned as too dangerous even for them to contemplate. There are curiously few returning elements, besides Death, Susan, the Death of Rats and Igor, and even Nanny Ogg's appearance is quite different from usual.

Subtext: Pratchett has played with time before – in *Wyrd Sisters* a whole period of time is removed to allow a character to grow up, in *Pyramids* the flaring of the pyramids brings past and present into collision, the primeval dawn of *The Last Continent.* The Trousers of Time recur at various points in the Discworld series, along with time travel in the Johnny Maxwell Trilogy. Somewhere behind this, then, is quantum thingummies, especially in the manipulation of time by the History Monks, and chaos theory.

But there's also the sense of historical process here, which has been apparent over the previous two or three Discworld novels. Aside from the historical setting of *Small Gods* and the gap in *Wyrd Sisters*, the events described in the Discworld series probably unfold over a couple of decades; Rincewind's exiles and return, Susan's birth and coming of age, Magrat's marriage and motherhood, Vimes and Carrot's careers in the watch all offer historical development and continuity, if not necessarily the same continuity. Now with claxes, c-commerce and the printing press there is the sense that the city of Ankh-Morpork has progressed from medieval to Renaissance to industrial nineteenth-century conurbation. One of the important factors of the progress of the nineteenth century was the unification of space and time. Whereas once peasants set their lives by the sun and let the minutes and seconds take care of themselves, innovations such as the telegraph and the railway meant that time needed to be fixed more precisely, and timezones were imposed upon areas, with 'natural,' cyclical, instinctive time usurped by the tyranny of the clock and the timetable. Susan's classes explore the different possibilities of time.

At the same time (so to speak) the novel offers some space for resistance to this encroaching modernity. By calling the new novice Ludd, the Luddites who fought against the introduction of machines in the early industrial age are invoked. Jeremy's work on manufacturing the clock is aided by Igor, one of the undead patchwork assistants who have appeared in the last few novels and who invoke the mock Gothic of 1930s Universal horror films. Ironically, of course, the End of History is a very late 1980s idea (see for example Francis Fukuyama's *The End Of History And The Last Man*), which has passed its sell by date.

The Verdict: All the monastery sections are excellent, and the use of the idea of time is very impressive, along with a number of conceptual leaps we are asked to make along the way. Perhaps, though, the linkage of the various threads is a bit clumsy – although a case can be made for it being thematically right. 4/5.

And next? Titles listed for 2001 publication: *The Last Hero* (illustrated by Paul Kidby) and *The Amazing Maurice And His Educated Rodents* (you know, for kids). Titles are subject to change and projects fall behind schedule, so treat this paragraph with caution.

Chapter Three: Children's Fiction

The Bromeliad, The Johnny Maxwell Trilogy

The *Discworld* novels are read by people of all ages, and whilst the target audience is adult, there is very little within them which might upset a child. Most of the references to sexuality are couched in terms that will go over the head of most children – although it would probably bore them rather than shock them, children being much more resilient than adults in these matters. There is, of course, a smattering of swearing. But Pratchett has also written fiction for children which, like the best children's fiction from Lewis Carroll and AA Milne to Diana Wynne Jones and Philip Pullman, can be enjoyed by children of all ages (don't you hate that phrase?). The children's books divide into two trilogies, one featuring nomes, the other featuring Johnny Maxwell. In fact, by rights *The Carpet People* should also be discussed here rather than in Chapter One.

The Bromeliad

Aside from the *Discworld* series, there are problems in knowing how to refer to the series written by Terry Pratchett, although you could argue the toss as to whether it's the *Discworld* sequence or the *Discworld* series, and whether both words should be capitalised, and of course individual sequences within the *Discworld*, er, sequence cause problems – such as the Guards, City Guards or City Watch group of novels, and as to whether *Pyramids*, *Small Gods* and *Hogfather* form a trilogy...

Try that one again. Well, let's just say that there is a tendency to group his books together as they are produced, or as they are reproduced in omnibus volumes. There was a tendency at first to write of the *Truckers* trilogy, somehow privileging the first volume. Then the books themselves contain subtitles – *Diggers* is *The Second Book Of The Nomes* and *Wings* is *The Third Book Of The Nomes*. So obviously the omnibus volume would be called *The Book Of The Nomes*. Right?

Wrong. *The Bromeliad*. This was the title given to the Science Fiction Bookclub edition in 1993, and the 1998 Doubleday omnibus. Since it contains four letters of the title *The Iliad*, you'd imagine that it was going to be some heroic epic, which it is, of course. And *Brome* is close enough to nome to speculate that it was going to be called *Nomeliad*, until someone pointed out that it was a silly title.

It is only in *Diggers* that we learn what a bromeliad is: a kind of pineapple plant that often grows on another tree without taking any nourishment from the tree. Instead it captures water and plants and animals who die and decay within a pool formed by leaves arranged in a bowl-like shape. As a side effect of this curious arrangement some creatures, from micro-organisms to frogs, live their entire life cycles inside the plant without being aware of any outside world, or indeed, presumably, of the plant being aware of their presence. The trilogy begins with the arrival of some nomes at a department store occupied by a society of nomes, a society which is not aware of what there is Outside. By the end of it, even the nomes from Outside discover they've been living in a state of ignorance as to their extraterrestrial origins.

The nomes are like people – who they regard as stupid – but much smaller, and they live their lives at a much faster rate than humans do. Whilst starting off looking like a fantasy trilogy, given the natural association of nomes with gnomes, it is obviously science fiction. Of course, it probably ought to be viewed as a mixture of the two since children have hazier ideas about genre and are less worried by authors breaking the rules.

Truckers

Published: London: Doubleday, 1989.

Location: A department store, Blackbury and environs.

Story: Masklin, Grimma and Granny Morkie are members of a group of nomes who have been living under a motorway and who, by chance, find their way into a department store. The store is inhabited by a hierarchical society of nomes who don't believe in the idea of Outside, but who do believe in Arnold Bros (est. 1905). Just as Masklin has convinced them that there is an Outside, they are badly in need of it, because the store is going to be knocked down. Can Masklin help them all to escape in time? And will the plan of driving out of there in a truck work?

Major Targets: Organised religion, stratified societies, sexism.

Subtext: Masklin is no leader. That is to say, he is not especially interested in power for his own benefit. He is interested in helping his fellow nomes to safety and inspiring them to help themselves in this quest. He is aided by his possession of a metal device known as the Thing, which is of some importance for some as yet unclear reason, and which can talk when in the region of electricity. Its advice is invaluable to Masklin.

Compare Masklin to the Abbot, who is the spiritual and secular leader of the nomes within the store. Because it has been decreed that there is no Outside, then no one can have possibly come from Outside. He literally cannot see Masklin. Or not publicly, anyway. In private, behind the scenes he is more pragmatic, more canny and can indeed grant them an interview without losing face. One feels the Abbot is as crafty as Patrician Vetinari from

Ankh-Morpork, except that he would not worry so much about losing face (although he would allow others to do the dirty work for him). The important thing is that the leader is strong – but a leader that doesn't bend occasionally is as bad as, say, one who is bent all the time.

The society the Abbot rules over is a stratified one, with each of the departments such as the Haberdasheri and the Stationeri being responsible for one skill. The danger is that the escape plan requires multitasking, and it is beneficial to all – and for all – that everyone can read. This becomes most controversial when Grimma wants to learn to read: she is, after all, a female nome and everyone knows that female nomes should not read or their heads will explode. No one has actually seen this happen, but it could happen, it could. Grimma has to face the double whammy of being female and an outsider, whereas Granny at least has age on her side. When Grimma does begin to read, she can feel her head expanding, as she gets direct access to the ideas which she has been denied all of her life.

Although nomes can read, they take most of what they read literally, and this is why they have created their own God, in the form of Arnold Bros (est. 1905), who the reader knows are brothers who established a store in the first years of the twentieth century. As a stabilising force, Arnold Bros (est. 1905) offers a regulatory framework of seasons, of sales, of reductions and of sage advice on notices. If the nomes are to mature, they need to be able to cope without even the idea of him. Various nomes see that having a God is useful to manipulate others. The danger comes in the reasoning behind that manipulation.

Of course, it must be admitted that Masklin has a crutch in the form of the Thing, which can answer all his questions for him, although he must work out precisely what the questions need to be. Occasionally the Thing even tells him that he must work it out for himself, and when there is no electricity all Masklin can do is use the Thing as a sounding board and rationalise himself.

It is interesting that Pratchett chose a narrative of the Outsider coming into a closed society; he could well have told a narrative of a closed society suddenly realising that there is another world outside their ken. But the society is so rigid, the presence of the God so overwhelming, that simply discovering that the store was going to be demolished would not lead to a conceptual breakthrough on the part of the nomes. The nomes – perhaps like us – need to be shown the way.

The Verdict: A great opening to a trilogy. 4/5

Diggers

Published: London: Doubleday, 1990.

Location: A quarry near Blackbury and its surroundings.

Story: The nomes have made a home for themselves in the disused quarry and they settle down to do whatever nomes do; eat and raise families mostly. Their idyll is shattered: they discover that the quarry is going to be used again for blasting and it is only a matter of time before they are discovered. The nomes are divided as to what to do for the best. Meanwhile the Thing is suggesting that the nomes are from another planet and that their mother ship is out there, somewhere, waiting. When Masklin discovers that Grandson, 39, a descendent of Arnold Bros (est. 1905), is launching something into space, another plan of escape suggests itself. But can they survive whilst Masklin travels to Florida?

Major Targets: There are references to *Gulliver's Travels*; religion is also a target.

Subtext: Whereas the centrepiece of *Truckers* is the co-operation of the characters as they learn to drive a truck, here the equivalent is a JCB, known to Dorcas as Jekub. Of course, this is less of a surprise than first time around, and correspondingly less is made of it.

Belief systems are again central. Can the nomes from the store survive out in the open without the reassuring presence of Arnold Bros (est. 1905) and all his works surrounding them? Well, it is difficult, but there's a suspicion that the message here has to be one of self-reliance without the crutch of a belief in a higher entity. It is important to believe in oneself and to back that up with intelligent actions. (The bases are loaded for us, of course, since we know there is no Arnold Bros (est. 1905).)

Nisodemus is set up as a bit of a straw, er, nome in this respect. Utterly convinced in the existence of Arnold Bros (est. 1905), Nisodemus believes that the God will protect the nomes from the onslaught of the humans. A notice on the gate telling them to go away is sufficient - the humans will understand and leave them alone. Something eminently practical like a good strong chain and padlock is too much like mistrusting God, and is disrespectful in the extreme. This is proven by the fact that the humans don't go away from the padlocked gate and rip up the notice. Arnold Bros (est. 1905) is obviously angry. Events reach a climax when he leads a group of nomes in an act of passive resistance, to stand in front of the trucks of the humans. The nomes see sense just in time, but the fate of Nisodemus is not recorded.

Better leadership qualities are displayed by Grimma, but then she does not desire power in the same way that Nisodemus takes it for himself. Since Masklin has to get to Florida to see Grandson, 39, he is unavoidably absent for much of the action. Masklin himself was a reluctant hero and an unwilling leader, but he had the power to get things done. Grimma has learnt from him, and is able to organise the nomes, more or less, despite a residual sexism within the former store community. (Granny Morkie, by contrast, wouldn't dream of letting sexism get in her way, just as she wouldn't dream of being a leader who gave orders. Rather like Granny Weatherwax from the *Discworld* series, she is a formidable enough presence that her requests are generally met.)

That is not to say that Grimma doesn't have her dark nights of the soul; there is one moment in particular where she gives way to despair, but an even bigger immediate crisis and her anger turns her round to fight again. This is important from a narrative point of view since there have to be obstacles to the nomes' actions for there to be drama, and Pratchett has made the humans so incomprehensible to the nomes that they cannot form much of the action. Foxes or rats, however, are much easier to describe.

It is in this volume that the Bromeliad are first mentioned and described, and it becomes a motif of becoming aware of our unknowing narrow-mindedness as to our own situations.

The Verdict: The traditional middle volume of a trilogy, which prolongs the plot until the climactic volume. 2/5

Wings

Published: London: Doubleday, 1990.

Location: At an airport near Blackbury, on Concorde, in Florida and in South America.

Story: Meanwhile... Masklin and a handful of other nomes decide to travel to Grandson, 39's launch, and smuggle themselves aboard Concorde. They have to evade detection, find food and make sure they end up at the right destination. Meanwhile... in South America, a frog discovers that there is a world outside the world in a plant it has grown up in.

Major Targets: A hint of Richard Branson hangs around Grandson, but only as a tycoon with teeth and a taste for the spectacular. And there are a few jokes at the expense of alien contact.

Subtext: Here Masklin is more of a free agent, because he doesn't have to take all of nomekind along with him, but he does have to cope with his companions, Abbot Gurder and Angalo, and the eternal problem of discovery. Pratchett established early in the *Discworld* series the ability of most people to edit out what they don't want to see; only children, wizards and witches seem to be able to see Death unless he wants them to see him. Similarly, since there can't possibly be four-inch-high nomes, most humans don't see them. But in the confined space of an aircraft or an airport, accidents happen. And sometimes it is necessary to make contact.

Speaking to Grandson Richard, 39, is a traumatic experience for Abbot Gurder: it is not as harrowing as meeting Arnold Bros (est. 1905) might have been, but it does come close to meeting a deity (albeit one who, given the thrust of the narrative, must bear some responsibility for demolishing their original department store in the name of progress). The fact that he has a hole in his sock becomes first a bit of a blow to Gurder's perception of the Divine nature, and then something to emulate. Different people cope in different ways, after all.

It also becomes clear that there are other nomes on Earth and indeed on other planets around other suns. This presents somewhat of a moral dilemma for the nomes: do the refugees have the right to take the ship for their own and to seek their own home? Or is it the property of all nomekind, wherever they are on the planet?

Meanwhile, in South America, a frog emerges from a Bromeliad, and discovers what its home looks like from the outside, indeed discovers that there is an outside. The frog's exploration intercuts with Masklin's quest. Just to make the link clear, Masklin reminds us that Grimma had read about such things. And as the spaceship leaves Earth (at the risk of ruining what is obviously going to be the ending) the Earth itself is a Bromeliad.

The Verdict: A bit of an open-ended ending, and some might find the use of the frogs heavy-handed. 3/5

The Johnny Maxwell Trilogy

These books are all set in Blackbury in the 1990s and feature Johnny Maxwell, child of a broken marriage, and his friends. In each of them Johnny, who should be a powerless child age twelve or thirteen, finds himself taking on responsibilities for others – aliens or the dead. The three books seem to stand alone, in that references are not made to the earlier books as the trilogy progresses, and Johnny's age isn't consistent with setting the books in the year of publication. Aha – the third volume includes the Trousers Of Time, a concept of the parallel world, and so these are presumably alternate or parallel Johnnies, in different versions of Blackbury, none of which, as far as we know, contain nomes.

Only You Can Save Mankind

Published: London: Doubleday, 1992.

Location: Blackbury and somewhere deep in space.

Story: Twelve-year-old Johnny Maxwell is playing the computer game *Only You Can Save Mankind* when the aliens surrender to him. Much to his surprise, he is now responsible for their safe passage to another zone of the galaxy, and he must defend them from their enemies – humans who are still playing the game. Back in the real world, he has all the problems of someone hitting their teens in the 1990s.

Major Targets: War (what is it good for?).

Subtext: There are two curious things about this book. Firstly it is Pratchett's least fantastical volume, featuring as it does the politics of the 1990s. And secondly, it is his most political book, even including *Jingo*.

Both of these statements need qualifying. Along with the world that turns out to be a spaceship, or a new Adam and Eve after an apocalypse, one of the most tiresome clichés of science fiction is the computer game which somehow turns out to be real - the *Dungeons & Dragons* game that has consequences in Fantasyland. That Johnny's encounter with the alien race ScreeWee turns out to be real could be a major turn-off. And yet Pratchett pulls it off. The iron logic that informs much of his work plays on the notion that aliens stay dead whereas humans come back from the dead, and the rest of Johnny's life offers the explanation of escapist fantasy.

Pratchett paints a very convincing picture of childhood in the 1990s, how half the class seem to be misfits, how skills are taught but can't be put into use, the fumblings of slang and coolness, and the alien ways of parents. Pratchett is able to encourage or endorse a resistance to sexism and racism using the way that Johnny interacts with Sigourney, who has been caught up in playing the game, and with his fat, skinhead and black friends. The alien captain is female, for a start (if creatures which are half-newt half-alligator have the same sexes as we do). The much more violent gunnery officer is male – but then Sigourney is much more gung-ho than Johnny has become. Under-age drinking, the hell of high-rise living in tower blocks which were slums only a couple of years after completion and joyriding are all included without Pratchett reading as though he is trying to be desperately relevant. And then there is the hell of dealing with parental psychological warfare – with each other or with Johnny. One character who has ambition thinks in terms of if he grows up, not when he grows up. Perhaps in naming the shop-keeper who owns the computer games shop in the Neil Armstrong Mall (previously mentioned in *Truckers*) Mr Patel, Pratchett puts a foot wrong: there must be other Pakistani names beyond that one. (Oh, and you probably wouldn't do Quadratic Equations at the age of twelve.)

And this all plays out against a backdrop of the Gulf War and Storming Norman Schwarzkopf, when television screens were filled with pictures of missile attacks more familiar from video games than war movies. Ironically, the social commentator Jean Baudrillard described the conflict (which he claims did not take place) as a virtual one, that it was like soldiers playing *Space Invaders*, hitting a button to fire a missile, and being isolated from the consequences.

There are a number of times when characters in the Discworld come to the brink of war – in *Pyramids* and *Jingo* war is averted by magical means. War is not approved of in the Pratchett oeuvre. But it is in this trilogy that he appears at his most pacifist – assuming that these are indeed Pratchett's own beliefs. (Would a pro-war book for children be published these days?)

Pratchett plays a marvellous set of tricks with language in which the recurring motif is the confusion of terminology. Earth is the home of humans, but it is also the translation of the ScreeWee's name for their own home planet. It is also made clear that ScreeWee is simply humanity's name for the ScreeWee; we never learn the ScreeWee's name for the ScreeWee. Presumably, though, it would be something akin to humanity. The irony of the novel's title – *Only You Can Save Mankind* – is that here mankind is the ScreeWee. Pratchett's shifting viewpoint – focusing in turn on Johnny, the alien captain and Sigourney – forces us to see more than one side to the situation.

The Verdict: A delight from beginning to end. 4/5

Johnny And The Dead

Published: London: Doubleday, 1993.

Location: Blackbury and, briefly, America.

Story: Johnny sees dead people. He sees them all the time. Oh, wrong story. Actually Johnny does see dead people, in Blackbury graveyard, down by the canal, and the dead are understandably worried about the news: the graveyard has been sold to a development company for five pence. Only Johnny can save the dead – but will the council listen to a thirteen-year-old?

Major Targets: Various movies of the undead, *Invasion Of The Body Snatchers* and local government corruption.

Subtext: There was at least one council in the 1980s that sold their grave-yards for a nominal fee, and rightly local people were scandalised. Here, in some ways, no one ought to care, since the only person who visits the grave-yard is Mrs Tachyon, and she's barking mad. Johnny sees it as his mission to do the right thing, and so he manages to take the matter to a local inquiry where he exposes the cynicism of the consultation exercise – the powers-that-be have long since made their minds up as to their course of action.

But hold on, is the graveyard really worth saving? No one seems to visit it, as I said, and not everything can be preserved forever. At the risk of giv-ing away some of the ending (look away now) not even the dead seem very attached to it now. The compromise that the living need graveyards more than the dead would be more convincing if we'd seen someone tending a grave, or talking to a lost loved one. Still, as is clear from the ending, most people don't know or care what they want until they are about to lose it.

Pratchett depicts the characters of the dead with great skill, as you'd expect; the Marxist is a particular joy and even sinister Mr Grimm is sensi-tively handled. Mr Atterbury is amusing as the kindly adult who helps Johnny take on the big guns. And Johnny's friends are a convincing cross-section of youth.

The Verdict: Not quite as politically savvy as the first volume in the tril-ogy – in fact at one point slightly (small c) conservative, but an entertaining yarn. 3/5

Johnny And The Bomb

Published: London: Doubleday, 1996.

Location: Blackbury, 1996 and 1941, and points in-between or alongside.

Story: Johnny finds the bag lady Mrs Tachyon has been attacked, and takes custody of her shopping trolley and her cat, Guilty. With Kirsty and his other friends he discovers that the trolley enables them to travel through time, back to 1941, and to the very day that bombs fell on Paradise Street, Blackbury with only two survivors, Adolf and Stalin the goldfish. Meanwhile a wealthy businessman is rushing to meet Johnny, a businessman who lived in Paradise Street during the Second World War.

Major Targets: The X-Files, care in the community, social workers, racism, time-travel books.

Subtext: Mrs Tachyon and her cat, Guilty, are key to this book. First introduced in *Johnny And The Dead*, everyone just dismisses her as a mad old biddy, a bag lady, who inexplicably hangs around the graveyard. Well, that latter is still inexplicable (although presumably she would know some of the inhabitants), but her madness is due to the fact that she travels in time with the aid of (or perhaps at the whim of) an otherwise ordinary Tesco shopping trolley. She is named for tachyons, hypothesised particles in advanced physics which travel faster than light and backwards in time.

The cat needs more explaining since it walks through walls. Of course, there is a Robert A Heinlein novel called *The Cat Who Walks Through Walls* (1985), although that probably shares a common source rather than being a source in itself. The scientist Schrödinger had a thought experiment to demonstrate the idea that light is both/either wave and/or particle until observed, in fact everything in the universe is only probable not actual until observed. Put a small piece of plutonium in a box, such that there is a fifty-fifty chance it will emit radiation in the next hour. Next rig up a phial of poison to leak if it detects poison. Finally place a cat in the box and close the lid. Question: is the cat dead or alive. Answer: yes. But it is only one or the other if the box is opened. The thought experiment is linked to all sorts of crazy ideas about quantum tunnelling and leaping, and things going from a to b without passing in-between.

Of course two things have to be noted, and they may well be linked: if the plutonium doesn't get you, being pretty poisonous in itself, the cat will. Have you ever tried putting a cat in a box? And even if you succeed, and retire to a safe distance, dripping with blood, the yowls from the damn thing will make it pretty clear what state the cat is in.

Where was I? Anyway, this branch of physics allows the possibility of alternate or parallel universes, created by events going different ways. You go back in time, kill your grandfather and you find yourself in a universe where you haven't been born. Which could prove embarrassing but goes some way to dealing with paradoxes. When Johnny and his friends go back in time they have to strike a balance between altering their history and thus their future, and getting things done which would have got done anyway, because, er, they did it in the first place. Some things may be better for short-term gain, but have long-term consequences.

Whilst Johnny is the centre of the narrative, his friends have their own problems. Yo-less witnesses first-hand the racial prejudice of the past – ironic given the unstated rationale of the Second War to fight anti-Semitic actions. Kirsty points out how sensibilities have changed over the years, but she is less blasé when she is the victim of the sexism of the period, even though sensibilities have changed over time. Meanwhile Bigmac's fashion sense, notably a camouflage coat and swastikas as subcultural marker, denotes him as a possible German spy and member of the Hitler Youth. Our actions and our tastes have consequences.

Alongside such serious matters, Pratchett tells a story of time travel and paradoxes with much relish, and it is one of his most complicated narratives. He sets up a section where one of the characters remains behind in the past and grows up (and hints at another example of this), and then erases it with another section where the character is rescued. By the end of the book, they're no longer in the same universe as they started. But it will do. Most of the characters have forgotten what has happened, the typical response of Pratchett's characters to events or entities they can't comprehend.

The Verdict: The finest of the children's books. 5/5

Chapter Four: Collaborations

The Unadulterated Cat, Good Omens, The Discworld Companion, The Maps, The Science Of Discworld, Nanny Ogg's Cookbook.

The Unadulterated Cat:
A Campaign For Real Cats

Credits: Terry Pratchett. Illustrations by Gray Jolliffe.

Who He? Gray Jolliffe is the cartoonist who did the *Wicked Willie* books with Peter Mayle.

Published: London: Gollancz, 1989.

Summary: A description of what real cats are like and should be, and some advice for dealing with them – or rather letting them get on with it.

Subtext: Real cats are not the pampered pedigree beasts that appear on commercials for expensive cat food out of square tins. Real cats aren't pedigree, they don't even know who their parents are. Real cats don't eat out of a bowl with their name on it. Real cats might eat out of a bowl labelled 'CAT', or rather from the floor next to the bowl. They are not mass-produced with genetic purity, but individuals.

A year after Pratchett gave us Greebo, he describes the true nature of these allegedly domesticated beasts and how to treat them, what to name them (nothing you'd be embarrassed to shout out of your back door at night), gives an analysis of the types of cat, imagines cats lost in alternate worlds and gives advice on feeding etiquette.

The Verdict: Not as funny (or as useful) as Simon Bond's *101 Uses For A Dead Cat*. 2/5

Good Omens: The Nice And Accurate Prophecies
Of Agnes Nutter, Witch

Credits: Terry Pratchett and Neil Gaiman, or Neil Gaiman and Terry Pratchett on US editions.

Who He?: Neil Gaiman was born in 1960 and is best known for his work scripting comics, most notably *The Sandman* series from 1988. His first book, co-edited with Kim Newman, was a collection of bad quotations from SF *Ghastly Beyond Belief* (1985). He also wrote *Don't Panic: The Official Hitchhiker's Guide To The Galaxy Companion* (1988). The story is that Gaiman and Pratchett were both owners of modems and the novel emerged from them trying to find something to do with such a device; the novel was apparently more successful than their use of the modem, as they switched to swapping discs rather quickly. Much brainstorming was done by phone. Pratchett wrote most of the bits with Adam and the Them, and Gaiman produced the bits with the Four Horsepersons. About two thirds of the book is Pratchett's, in part because Gaiman was busy on *The Sandman*.

Published: London: Gollancz, 1990. (The US (Workman) edition is revised, in part to make some of the specific references clearer for the American market. The 1991 Corgi edition offers further refinements.)

Location: Southern England – London, South Oxfordshire and the M40 corridor; briefly in foreign territories and the Garden of Eden.

Story: Eleven years ago the Anti-Christ was born and, due to mismanagement, was not swapped with the baby of the American ambassador, but rather with that of Mr and Mrs Young, a rather nice couple who live somewhere in South Oxfordshire. So, with Armageddon a few hours away, it's rather embarrassing for all concerned that they've temporarily mislaid the spawn of Satan, and good angel Aziraphale and fallen angel Crowley are beginning to have second thoughts about the whole business. The end is also anticipated by Anathema Device, a descendent of Agnes Nutter who wrote a famous (and notoriously accurate) book of prophecies and Witchfinders Newton Pulsifer and Shadwell. Meanwhile, the Four Horsepersons of the Apocalypse are about to ride their motorbikes north...

Major Targets: The *Omen* cycle, particularly the first two films, the Apocalypse in general and Four Horsemen in particular, prophecies – of Nostrodamus and Joanna Southcott – and medieval superstitions. The M25. Americans.

Cameos: Death: Presumably a different Death, but still speaking in capitals, along with his companions Famine, War and Pollution. *Witches:* Agnes Nutter for one, and others pursued by the Witchfinders.

Subtext: Pratchett has usually shied away from the end of the world – that's to come in *Discworld* novels published after this one. In the meantime there's fun to be had at the expense of the arcane language of soothsayers and how it often needs an event to have happened before the prophecy can be explained. Bits and pieces of *Revelations* can also be brought to bear.

The kids – including the Anti-Christ – and their gang are dry runs for the central characters in the Johnny Maxwell trilogy, even down to the token girl who fits in rather too well to be entirely convincing. We probably hear more about them than we get to see in action, which is a shame, although as they cycle into the American airbase at the climax there's a neat reference to *ET: The Extra-Terrestrial*. The happy ending that follows is just a little too neat.

Aside from the Four Horsepersons – and the gang of Hell's Angels who aspire to follow in their footsteps, er, hoofmarks, tyre treads, er, wake – the best sequences involve Crowley and Aziraphale. Not only does Crowley have a lighter side to his demonic personality (he didn't ask to be fallen) but Aziraphale has a darker side. There's also a chance for a debate about the nature of free will – obviously Adam and Eve were set up in the Garden of Eden.

The Verdict: A bit too farcical in places, and the humour seems a little forced (especially the footnotes). Still, the Four Horsepersons are fun, and Crowley is worth a second look. 3/5

The Discworld Companion

Credits: Terry Pratchett and Stephen Briggs.

Who He?: Born in 1951, and now resident in Oxfordshire, Stephen Briggs is a civil servant who got interested in the Discworld through his amateur dramatics. Someone loaned him *Wyrd Sisters* and he adapted it for performance, followed by *Mort*, *Guards! Guards!* and *Men At Arms*. He also convinced Pratchett that a map of Ankh-Morpork was possible (see below) and the arguments over details led to perceiving the need for a reference book.

Published: London: Gollancz, 1994; revised edition 1997.

Summary: After introductions by Pratchett and Briggs, a cross-referenced A to Z to characters, places and objects on Discworld, followed by a history of the *Discworld* phenomenon in book form, on stage, in clay, on computer, in translation and finally a composite interview.

The Subtext: What's to say? If you are a serious fan of Discworld you should buy this; if you dip in and out of the novels or only read them every year or so this will fill in gaps. It also has seeds for future novels; the 1994 edition mentions a William de Worde who doesn't appear until *The Truth*.

Verdict: Sometimes the book's tendency to alphabeticise by surname (which it doesn't always do) means that some characters known by their first names, or indeed other names, are hard to find. Stick with it, you'll find the entry eventually. 4/5

The Streets Of Ankh-Morpork

Being A Concise And Possibly Even Accurate Mapp Of The Discworld:
Including Unseen University And Environs! Also Finest Assortment Of Ave-
nues, Lanes, Squares And Alleys For Your Walking Pleasure.

Credits: Devised by Stephen Briggs. Assisted by Terry Pratchett.

Published: London: Corgi, 1993.

Summary: A map of Ankh-Morpork, which is a circular city shaped
rather like an onion. The river Ankh runs from top to bottom on the map,
which is odd since we (well, I) generally think of rivers as running East-
West or vice versa. London. Newcastle. Bristol. Glasgow. Melbourne. If
you turn the map ninety degrees clockwise it would look rather like London,
complete with Isle of Dogs. Around the edges of the map are the Coats of
Arms of the various Guilds, which are reproduced in *The Discworld Companion*. The accompanying book has an introduction from Terry Pratchett,
discussing how he never had a map, and another one from Stephen Briggs
about how he went about drawing one. Fortunately the city is vague and
large enough that there aren't too many points of discontinuity, but even so
it must have been a mammoth task. The booklet lists various places marked
on the map.

This is for completists only, I'd say; it's too brown-green an object to
stick on the wall, and when would you want to look at it?

The Discworld Mapp

Being The Onlie True & Mostlie Accurate Mappe Of The Fantastyk &
Magical Dyscworlde.

Credits: Devised by Terry Pratchett and Stephen Briggs. Drawn by
Stephen Player.

Published: London: Corgi, 1995.

Summary: Another circular space is mapped, with the turtle visible
below it. All the countries mentioned in the books can be located on the
map. The mapping of the map coincided with the writing of *The Lost Continent* and could thus take XXXX's position into account. The locations
which figure most often are numbered rather than marked. Again, there is a
certain drabness about the map which I don't feel with real maps, like Ord-
nance Survey Maps for example.

Of course, in the epigraph to *Sourcery* Pratchett had written that there
was no map of Discworld and that we were free to draw our own. To me,
that sounded like a gentle send-up of the verisimilitudinous tendencies of
much genre fantasy (it must be fantasy – there's a map!). In the accompanying booklet to this previously non-existent map, Pratchett mentions that

people *did* and sent him copies. So, an exercise in reducing fan mail? Perhaps. After all, there are more possibilities for geographical errors as the series progresses and the resultant letters of complaint to point out these errors. At the same time, it's intriguing to see Pratchett's comments to Stephen Briggs about rainfall patterns – even if it is a protective measure, Pratchett clearly wants his world to work on scientific principles, or at least not contradict basic geography. (And geology – Ankh-Morpork is built on loam).

The map also includes some accounts of explorers' voyages – including Ponce da Quirm (from *Eric*), Lars Larsnephew and Lady Alice Venturi. There are also accounts of the theory of plate tectonic. And a funny joke about gardening. The text is amusing, but still for completists I'd say.

A Tourist Guide To Lancre

A Discworld Mapp Including A Pyctorial Guide To The Lancre Fells And A Description Of A Picturefque And Charming Walk In Thys Charming And Hospital Country.

Credits: Devised by Terry Pratchett and Stephen Briggs. View of Lancre by Paul Kidby.

Published: London: Corgi, 1998.

Summary: The booklet with this map shows real signs of inventiveness in presenting us with, and fleshing out materials from, a number of the witch books. Gytha Ogg's voice, typographical errors and all, is used to tell us about the highlights of this rural community, the shops, the people, the services and so forth. Meanwhile there is an account of Eric Wheelwright – the Discworld's answer to fell walker Alfred Wainwright – and his exploration of the area, as well as one of his accounts of a walk around Lancre. Wheelwright was rarely to be seen without a trusty set of wire cutters to remove fences across rights of way; back in the real world the right to roam was a political issue in late 1990s Britain.

The map itself is of a clear vertiginous region, with Lancre apparently perched high on cliffs above great gorges carved out by the rivers, and it is overlooked by the Ramtop Mountains. Over thirty sites of interest are picked out on the map itself, plus enlargements of Lancre town itself and Lancre Castle. The map screams fantasy landscape, albeit in rather mute muddy colours. Around the edge are pictures of Ogg and Weatherwax (the latter perhaps a little too ugly for the initial description in *Equal Rites*, but round enough in face) and of Queen Magrat – but not of Agnes/Perdita or even the Ogg clan.

Death's Domain

A Discworld Mapp.
Credits: Devised by Terry Pratchett and Paul Kidby.
Published: London: Corgi, 1999.

Summary: Another large-scale piece, purple rather than black, and showing Death's house, a maze, ornamental gardens, the vegetable gardens, corn fields in the distance and around the edge, picture of Death, Albert, a peacock, a raven, the Death of Rats and presumably Susan. Mort and Ysabell are nowhere to be seen.

The accompanying booklet begins with an overview of Death, along with Albert, Mort, Ysabell and Susan, before moving on to a description of the Domain, complete with quotes from the novels. There is a section on black (the iridescent black of a starling's wing) and finally on the house, including a quotation from W H J Whittleby's *Guide To Impossible Buildings*.

Here's an irony, though. It's the best looking of all the maps – to the extent that it is a map rather than an annotated illustration, but the dullest text, bringing together little more than what we know already.

The Science Of Discworld

Credits: Terry Pratchett, Ian Stewart and Jack Cohen.
Who They?: Ian Stewart is a mathematician, who has published a number of very accessible books on the subject. Jack Cohen is a biologist, who has published on the subject, and has given many talks at science fiction conventions on evolution and biology.
Published: London: Ebury Press, 1999.
Location: Unseen University, Ankh-Morpork and Roundworld.
Story: A project by Ponder Stibbons to split the thaum produces too much magical energy, magic which needs to be used up before it engulfs the Discworld. HEX suggests the Roundworld project, creating a new universe where magic doesn't work. Before long (a couple of million years) they've made a spherical planet, and life is evolving. Someone needs to take a closer look; who better than Rincewind. Meanwhile we are treated to a description of the history of Earth from the big bang to the present and beyond.
Major Targets: Science, scientific curiosity – but also ignorance and superstition. There's one or two pot-shots at the politics of university funding and organisation.
Cameos: Death: Discussed briefly in one of the science sections. *The Librarian:* Takes an interest in the new planet. *Wizards:* Engaged in playful magical experimentation. *Greebo:* Mentioned in relation to Schrödinger's

cat. *Unseen University:* Setting for the new universe and planet. *CMOT Dibbler:* Mentioned in passing.

Subtext: There are a number of spin-off books from popular media SF with science or physics in the title – *Star Trek* and *X-Files* in particular – which form excuses for popular retellings of the cutting edge of scientific speculation. In part because of Pratchett's direct involvement in the project, this one is in the flavour of the original as science and fiction meld.

The *Discworld* series offers us a chance to observe similarities and differences between a fantasy world and our own, but the logic of Discworld also allows us to view our own world through different eyes. The Wizards of the Discworld's Unseen University have become so familiar and real to us that we sort of trust their judgements - we can certainly understand how they react to our world.

Occasionally Cohen and Stewart (who presumably are responsible between them for the science chapters) are able to use quotations from the *Discworld* series to highlight points about science, but mostly they write in a clear, jargon-free language on topics such as the big bang, plate tectonics, evolution, the extinction of the dinosaurs and so forth.

Whilst they display the odd anti-spiritual prejudice (this is a history of the world which has no space for God) they are not quite as pro-science as you might expect. Or rather, they refuse to see science as a uniform, monolithic entity which explains everything – since it is the provisional narrative, even lie, told by scientists to the best of their ability. Science has been wrong before – or perhaps scientists have been wrong before – and may be wrong again. Science will one day be able to explain the whole universe, form a theory of everything, but in the meantime there are approximations and hypotheses. The writers are also careful to show how selective use of evidence – on the part of scientists who want a breakthrough or on the part of journalists who want a story – can give a false picture of the universe.

The Verdict: A very accessible primer on science – cosmology, quantum mechanics, evolution and DNA – intercut with a rather slender narrative on the evolution of a planet. 3/5

Nanny Ogg's Cookbook

Including Recipes, Items Of Antiquarian Lore, Improving Observations Of Life, Good Advice For Young People On The Threshold Of The Adventure That Is Marriage, Notes On Etiquette & Many Other Helpful Observations That Will Not Offend The Most Delicate Sensibilities.

Credits: Terry Pratchett, Stephen Briggs, Tina Hannan and illustrations by Paul Kidby.

Published: London: Transworld, 1999.

Summary: A Discworld equivalent of *Mrs Beaton's Cookbook*, complete with recipes and etiquette advice.

Subtext: Back in *Maskerade* Nanny Ogg has a book published, a cookbook full of erotic recipes and advice. This is presumably meant to be it, although it was actually *The Joye Of Snacks* by A Lancre Witch. Recipe books sell like hot cakes, although people never quite get around to making the recipes, and are usually a sign that Technical Manuals (the Watch's code and the rules of Ankh-Morpork?), cross-sections and dictionaries of made-up languages are not far behind.

The Verdict: I hear barrels being scraped. Or saucepans. 1/5

Reference Materials

Books, Short Works, Collaborations, Scripts And Comics, Criticism, Videos, DVDs, CDs, Websites

Works

Below is an alphabetical list of the first editions of Pratchett's novels as published in Britain. It is beyond the scope of the essential to keep track of all the paperbacks (mostly published by Corgi a year after the hardback), book club editions and translations of these books. For a period the *Discworld* books were also published in compact editions, apparently unabridged. Most of the books have been made into abridged audiobooks, read by Tony Robinson. Complete versions have been issued by ISIS.

Books by Terry Pratchett

1998. *Carpe Jugulum*. London: Doubleday.

1971. *The Carpet People*. Gerrards Cross: Colin Smythe.

1992. *The Carpet People*. London: Doubleday.

1983. *The Colour Of Magic*. Gerrards Cross: Colin Smythe.

1976. *The Dark Side Of The Sun*. London: Colin Smythe.

1990. *Diggers*. London: Doubleday.

1987. *Equal Rites*. London: Gollancz in association with Colin Smythe.

1990. *Eric*. London: Gollancz. Illustrated by Josh Kirby.

1996. *Feet Of Clay*. London: Gollancz.

1999. *The Fifth Elephant*. London: Doubleday.

1989. *Guards! Guards!* London: Gollancz.

1996. *Hogfather*. London: Gollancz.

1994. *Interesting Times*. London: Gollancz.

1997. *Jingo*. London: Gollancz.

1996. *Johnny And The Bomb*. London: Doubleday.

1993. *Johnny And The Dead*. London: Doubleday.

1998. *The Last Continent*. London: Doubleday.

1986. *The Light Fantastic*. London: Colin Smythe.

1992. *Lords And Ladies*. London: Gollancz.

1995. *Maskerade*. London: Gollancz.

1993. *Men At Arms*. London: Gollancz.

1987. *Mort*. London: Gollancz in association with Colin Smythe.

1990. *Moving Pictures*. London: Gollancz.

1992. *Only You Can Save Mankind*. London: Doubleday.

1989. *Pyramids*. London: Gollancz.

1991. *Reaper Man*. London: Gollancz.

1992. *Small Gods*. London: Gollancz.

1994. *Soul Music*. London: Gollancz.

1988. *Sourcery*. London: Gollancz in association with Colin Smythe.

1981. *Strata*. Gerrards Cross: Colin Smythe.

2000. *The Truth*. London: Doubleday UK.

1989. *Truckers*. London: Doubleday.

1989. *The Unadulterated Cat*. London: Gollancz. Illustrated by Gray Jolliffe.

1990. *Wings*. London: Doubleday.

1991. *Witches Abroad*. London: Gollancz.

1988. *Wyrd Sisters*. London: Gollancz.

Short Works

1990. '#ifdefDEBUG + 'world/enough' + 'time'.' *Digital Dreams*, edited by David Barrett. London: NEL.

1987. '20p With Envelope And Seasonal Greeting.' *Time Out* (Christmas).

1988. 'Final Reward.' *G.M.* (October).

1990. 'Hollywood Chickens.' *More Tales From The Forbidden Planet*, edited by Roz Kaveney. London: Titan.

1988. 'Incubust.' *The Drabble Project*, edited by Rob Meades and David B Wake. Harold Wood: Beccon.

1993. 'Let There Be Dragons.' *The Bookseller* (11 June).

1965. 'Night Dweller.' *New Worlds* 49.

1995. 'Once And Future.' *Camelot*, edited by Jane Yolen. New York: Philomel Books.

1963. 'The Hades Business.' *Science-Fantasy* 20. Reprinted 1965 in *The Unfriendly Future*, edited by Tom Boardman Jr. London: Four Square Books/New English Library.

1998. 'The Sea And Little Fishes.' *Legends: Masters Of Fantasy*, edited by Robert Silverberg. London: HarperCollins.

1991. 'The Secret Book Of The Dead.' *Now We Are Sick: An Anthology Of Nasty Verse*, edited by Neil Gaiman and Stephen Jones. Dreamhaven Books.

1993. 'Theatre Of Cruelty.' *WHS Bookcase* 45.

1992. 'Troll Bridge.' *After The King*, edited by Martin H Greenberg. London: Pan.

1989. 'Turntables Of The Night.' *Hidden Turnings*, edited by Diana Wynne Jones. London: Mammoth.

Collaborations

Briggs, Stephen. 1993. *The Streets of Ankh-Morpork*. London: Corgi.

Briggs, Stephen. 1995. *The Discworld Companion*. London: Gollancz.

Briggs, Stephen. 1995. *The Discworld Mapp*. London: Corgi.

Briggs, Stephen. 1997. *Discworld's Unseen University Diary, 1998*; illustrated by Paul Kidby. London: Gollancz.

Briggs, Stephen. 1997. *The Discworld Companion – Updated*. London: Vista.

Briggs, Stephen. 1998. *Discworld's Ankh-Morpork City Watch Diary 1999*; illustrated by Paul Kidby. London: Gollancz.

Briggs, Stephen. 1998. *Terry Pratchett's Maskerade*. London: Samuel French.

Briggs, Stephen and Kidby, Paul. 1998. *A Tourist Guide To Lancre*. London: Corgi.

Briggs, Stephen. 1999. *Discworld Assassins' Guild Yearbook And Diary 2000*; illustrated by Paul Kidby. London: Gollancz.

Briggs, Stephen. 2000. *The Discworld Fools' Guild Yearbook And Diary 2001*; illustrated by Paul Kidby. London: Gollancz.

Briggs, Stephen, Hannan, Tina and Kidby, Paul. 1999. *Nanny Ogg's Cookbook*. London: Doubleday.

Gaiman, Neil. 1990. *Good Omens: The Nice And Accurate Prophecies Of Agnes Nutter. Witch: A Novel*. London: Gollancz.

Kidby, Paul. 1996. *The Pratchett Portfolio*. London: Gollancz.

Kidby, Paul. 1999. *Death's Domain*. London: Corgi.

Kirby, Josh. 1989. *The Josh Kirby Poster Book, Inspired By Terry Pratchett's Discworld Novels*. London: Corgi.

Stewart, Ian and Cohen, Jack. 1999. *The Science Of Discworld*. London: Ebury Press.

A Note For Collectors

Copies of first editions of novels by Terry Pratchett can exchange for prices much greater than their cover price. You should be warned that some dealers are less than scrupulous about how they describe the condition of their stock; you can't check this online. This is a rough guide to prices of first editions. It should be noted that some specialist science fiction dealers are likely to be cheaper than Internet sources or antiquarians. The considerable margins listed below are between the lowest price you can expect to pay in the real world and the highest the most expensive I've seen in cyberspace. I recommend you go for the lower price...

The early Colin Smythe Ltd editions are obviously the most valuable, with copies of *The Carpet People* going for £250-£650, probably around £300, *The Dark Side Of The Sun* for £200-£500, *Strata* £100-£200 and *The Light Fantastic* anything from £250-£2500. The biggie is *The Colour Of Magic*, of which 506 copies were printed, with the price in the region of £1000-£9,000 for a second-hand copy. The Gollancz edition *Discworld* novels from *Equal Rites* to *Wyrd Sisters* are generally priced from £25-£250, and from *Guards! Guards!* to *Soul Music* in the £20-£100 region. Later volumes, including the Doubleday editions, can usually be picked up for £20 or less. The exception to this is the hardback of *Eric*, which I've seen at £250. The children's books vary in value, from £10 to £60. Presumably these will become rarer as children's books. *Good Omens* is around the £30-£100 mark.

Scripts And Comics

Briggs, Stephen. 1996. *Terry Pratchett's Mort – The Play*. London: Corgi.

Briggs, Stephen. 1996. *Johnny And The Dead*. Oxford: Oxford University Press.

Briggs, Stephen. 1996. *Terry Pratchett's Wyrd Sisters – The Play*. London: Corgi.

Briggs, Stephen. 1997. *Terry Pratchett's Guards! Guards! – The Play*. London: Corgi.

Briggs, Stephen. 1997. *Terry Pratchett's Men At Arms – The Play*. London: Corgi.

Briggs, Stephen. 1999. *Terry Pratchett's Carpe Jugulum: A Play*. London: Samuel French.

Hibbert, Jimmy. 1998. *Wyrd Sisters: The Illustrated Screenplay*. London: Corgi.

Higgins, Graham. Adapted by Stephen Briggs. 2000. *Guards! Guards! A Discworld Big Comic*. London: Gollancz.

Higgins, Graham. 1994. *Mort, A Discworld Big Comic*. London: VP Graphics.

Jameson, Martin [uncredited on cover]. 1997. *Soul Music: The Illustrated Screenplay*. London: Corgi.

Rockwell, Scott. 1992. *Terry Pratchett's The Colour Of Magic: The Graphic Novel*, illustrated by Steven Ross. London: Corgi.

Rockwell, Scott. 1993. *Terry Pratchett's The Light Fantastic: The Graphic Novel*, illustrated by Steven Ross and Joe Bennet. London: Corgi.

Criticism

Butler, Andrew M. 1996. 'Terry Pratchett And The Comedic Bildungsroman.' *Foundation: The Review Of Science Fiction* 67. An article which looks at the carnivalesque as described by Russian theorist Mickail Bakhtin, and how it can be seen as anticipating Death in *Mort*. It is unclear, according to Pratchett, whether this is very clever or a spoof. The question remains unanswered. The sections not dealing with the Bildungsroman (the coming-of-age narrative) are incorporated into 'Theories Of Humour' in *Terry Pratchett: Guilty Of Literature*.

Butler, Andrew M, James, Edward and Mendlesohn, Farah, eds. 2000. *Terry Pratchett: Guilty Of Literature*. Reading: SFF. A collection of essays on Terry Pratchett's fiction. After an editorial preface and an introduction by David Langford disguised as a foreword, the chapters divide into two types: thematic and sequence. Themes include coming of age (John Clute), theories of humour (Andrew M Butler), faith and ethics (Farah Mendlesohn) and mapping (Matthew Hills). The sequences covered are the children's books (Cherith Baldry), the Unseen University (Penelope Hill), the Librarian (Andy Sawyer, a librarian himself, but strictly human), the Witches (Karen Sayer), the City Watch (Edward James) and Death (Nickianne Moody). The essays range in difficulty from the densely argued (Butler and Hills) to the literary appreciative (James and Baldry) and take in literature, history, culture and so forth. Something for everyone although, as one particularly perceptive reviewer noted, it helps if you've read some Pratchett.

Clute, John and Grant, John, eds. 1997. *The Encyclopaedia Of Fantasy*. London: Orbit. Entry on Pratchett is written by David Langford and forms a useful overview of his work.

Clute, John. 1990. 'The Big Sellers 3: Terry Pratchett.' *Interzone* 33. Probably the first piece of anything like sustained criticism on Pratchett, which notes the tendency of the early books (by no means all of them) to use a young protagonist who grows up in the process of the novel, and then is forgotten about. Clute also considers the idea of comedy. Revised and much expanded as 'Coming Of Age' in *Terry Pratchett: Guilty Of Literature*.

James, Edward. 1994. *Science Fiction In The Twentieth Century*. Oxford: Oxford University Press.

Kincaid, Paul. 1995. *A Very British Genre: A Short History Of British Fantasy And Science Fiction*. Folkestone: British Science Fiction Association. Two histories of science fiction which also take in fantasy en route. James covers world SF, but with a bias to the American. Kincaid's book is a pamphlet originally produced for the 1995 Worldcon in Glasgow, which gives a rather breathless history of fantastic literature in Britain. I mean, trying to cover a huge subject in 35,000 words. Who'd do something daft like that? Pratchett gets brief mentions in both.

Langford, David. 1996. *The Unseen University Challenge – Terry Pratchett's Discworld Quizbook*. London: Vista. Despite the title, it doesn't limit itself to the Discworld, although most of the book covers that part of Pratchett's oeuvre. The questions range from the bleeding obvious to the downright perversely difficult, although the book is rather torpedoed by the designer's decision to print most of the answers, the right way up, the right way round, right next to the questions. It's worth skimming through, since the award-winning David Langford is a great humorist himself (check out www.ansible.demon.co.uk) and dangerously erudite. Somewhat to the chagrin of Mr Pratchett himself, one presumes, Langford will insist in pointing out the Discworld's literary borrowings.

Simpson, MJ, ed. May 1997. *SFX Presents The Authorised Terry Pratchett's Discworld Magazine*. One issue by Future Publishing: 'Ye Editor, Mr M. J. Simpson, Publyshed by Dibbler Press, Ankh-Morpork'.

Videos

Truckers (1992)

13 x 11-minute episodes. Transmitted: 10 January – 3 April 1992.
Director: Jackie Cockle. Writer: Brian Trueman.
Starring: Joe McGann, Debra Gillette, Rosalie Williams, John Jardine, Edward Kelsey, Brian Trueman, Jimmy Hibbert.
Video is feature-length version: PAL format; ASIN: B00004CM0K; Catalogue Number: PTVID8026.

Johnny And The Dead (1995)

4 x 30-minute episodes. Transmitted: 4-25 April 1995.
Writers: Gerald Fox, Terry Pratchett, Lindsey Jenkins.
Starring: Andrew Falvey, George Baker, Brian Blessed, Jane Lapotaire.
PAL Format; 0630 10906-3.

Wyrd Sisters From Terry Pratchett's Discworld (1996)

147 Minutes. 6 x 30-minute episodes. Transmitted: 11 May-15 June 1997.
Director: Jean Flynn. Writer: Jimmy Hibbert.
Starring: Christopher Lee, Jane Horrocks, June Whitfield, Eleanor Bron.
PAL format; Box set; ASIN: B00004CV82; Catalogue Number: AST1046.

Soul Music From Terry Pratchett's Discworld (1996)

Released on video 12 May 1997.
Director: Jean Flynn. Writer: Martin Jameson.
Starring: Christopher Lee.
PAL format; Box set; ASIN: B00004CW4G; Catalogue Number: AST1047.

The traditional story is that the people who were going to film *Mort* wanted to lose the Death angle. Other attempts have no doubt been made to option the novels - Catalyst Television have the rights to *The Colour Of Magic* and *The Light Fantastic* - but have fallen through thanks to lack of money or a return of common sense. Further adaptations, for example, had been planned after *Truckers*, but Thames lost their franchise.

A recurring rumour is that *Good Omens* is to be filmed, directed by Terry Gilliam. The latest news is that the script will be co-written by Gilliam and Tony Grisoni and will be filmed in 2001. Don't believe a word of it until you see the trailers. Gilliam has a long line of great projects that never materialised or have been delayed by the studio.

DVDs

Wyrd Sisters

North America: Acorn Media / UK: Vision Video

Soul Music

North America: Acorn Media / UK: Vision Video

CDs

Dave Greenslade, *From The Discworld*. Themes for a number of books and songs 'The Shades Of Ankh-Morpork' and 'A Wizard's Staff Has A Knob On The End.' Virgin (UK:CDV 2738).

Keith Hopwood and Phil Bush, *Soul Music*. Music from the soundtrack with additional material. Pluto Music (TH 030746).

Websites

Transworld's Terry Pratchett Pages:

http://www.booksattransworld.co.uk/terrypratchett - This is a gateway to information about Terry Pratchett (but less than you'd glean from holding one of his books in your hand) and the ability to order some of the Doubleday hardbacks. I tried to access this site a number of times with Netscape but the computer threw its hands up in disgust; Internet Explorer seems more amenable, for what it was worth.

L-Space Website:

http://www.co.uk.lspace.org/ - Probably the largest Pratchett site, containing biographical materials, quotations, fan activity, artwork, merchandising, FAQs and so on. It also includes **The Annotated Pratchett File** (http://www.co.uk.lspace.org/books/apf/index.html) a giant archive of the references fans have spotted or think they have spotted in Pratchett's books. You can also find Christopher Bryant's undergraduate dissertation **Postmodern Parody In The Discworld Novels Of Terry Pratchett** (http://www.co.uk.lspace.org/books/postmodern-pratchett.html) and Pratchett's short story **Theatre Of Cruelty** (http://www.co.uk.lspace.org/books/misc/theatre-of-cruelty.html).

Colin Smythe Ltd. Terry Pratchett Pages:

http://www.colinsmythe.co.uk/authors/tp/index.html - Colin Smythe Ltd, a publisher based in Gerrards Cross, was for many years the publisher of Terry Pratchett. Then the success of the *Discworld* novels meant that Pratchett outgrew his publisher, and Colin Smythe became his agent.

Orangutan Foundation International:

http://www.orangutan.org/index.html **Orangutan Foundation United Kingdom**: http://www.orangutan.org.uk - The Librarian becoming an orangutan (or orang-utan) was just a throwaway joke, but the Librarian became one of Pratchett fans' favourite characters, going on to appear in almost all of the *Discworld* novels. Pratchett became aware of and concerned with the plight of the apes in the wild, and supports the charity which supports them.

The Discworld Monthly:

http://www.ufbs.co.uk/dwm/ - Site of *The Discworld Monthly*, a monthly newszine about Terry Pratchett.

Wossname:

http://www.egroups.com/message/WOSSNAME/ - The Newsletter of the North American Discworld Society.

The Essential Library

New: **Filming On A Microbudget** by Paul Hardy (£3.99)
      Terry Pratchett by Andrew M Butler (£3.99)
      The Hitchhiker's Guide by M J Simpson (£3.99)

Film: **Woody Allen** by Martin Fitzgerald (£3.99)
      Jane Campion by Ellen Cheshire (£2.99)
      John Carpenter by Colin Odell & Michelle Le Blanc (£3.99)
      Jackie Chan by Michelle Le Blanc & Colin Odell (£2.99)
      Joel & Ethan Coen by John Ashbrook & Ellen Cheshire (£3.99)
      David Cronenberg by John Costello (£3.99)
      Film Noir by Paul Duncan (£3.99)
      Terry Gilliam by John Ashbrook (£2.99)
      Heroic Bloodshed edited by Martin Fitzgerald (£2.99)
      Alfred Hitchcock by Paul Duncan (£2.99)
      Horror Films by Colin Odell & Michelle Le Blanc (£3.99)
      Krzysztof Kieslowski by Monika Maurer (£2.99)
      Stanley Kubrick by Paul Duncan (£2.99)
      David Lynch by Michelle Le Blanc & Colin Odell (£3.99)
      Steve McQueen by Richard Luck (£2.99)
      Marilyn Monroe by Paul Donnelley (£3.99)
      The Oscars® by John Atkinson (£3.99)
      Brian De Palma by John Ashbrook (£2.99)
      Sam Peckinpah by Richard Luck (£2.99)
      Ridley Scott by Brian J Robb (£3.99)
      Slasher Movies by Mark Whitehead (£3.99)
      Vampire Films by Michelle Le Blanc & Colin Odell (£2.99)
      Orson Welles by Martin Fitzgerald (£2.99)
      Billy Wilder by Glenn Hopp (£3.99)

TV: **Doctor Who** by Mark Campbell (£3.99)

Books: **Cyberpunk** by Andrew M Butler (£3.99)
      Philip K Dick by Andrew M Butler (£3.99)
      Noir Fiction by Paul Duncan (£2.99)

Culture:**Conspiracy Theories** by Robin Ramsay (£3.99)

Available at all good bookstores, or send a cheque to: **Pocket Essentials (Dept TP), 18 Coleswood Rd, Harpenden, Herts, AL5 1EQ, UK**. Please make cheques payable to 'Oldcastle Books.' Add 50p postage & packing for each book in the UK and £1 elsewhere.

US customers can send $6.95 plus $1.95 postage & packing for each book to: **Trafalgar Square Publishing, PO Box 257, Howe Hill Road, North Pomfret, Vermont 05053, USA**. e-mail: tsquare@sover.net

Customers worldwide can order online at **www.pocketessentials.com**.